THE WORK OF ART

CULTURE AND ECONOMIC LIFE

THE WORK OF ART

Value in Creative Careers

ALISON GERBER

STANFORD UNIVERSITY PRESS
STANFORD, CALIFORNIA

Stanford University Press
Stanford, California

Printed in the United States of America on acid-free, archival-quality paper

Library of Congress Cataloging-in-Publication Data

Names: Gerber, Alison, author.
Title: The work of art : value in creative careers / Alison Gerber.
Description: Stanford, California : Stanford University Press, 2017. |
 Series: Culture and economic life | Includes bibliographical references
 and index. | Description based on print version record and CIP data
 provided by publisher; resource not viewed.
Identifiers: LCCN 2017028663 (print) | LCCN 2017030513 (ebook) |
 ISBN 9781503604032 (electronic) | ISBN 9780804798310 (cloth : alk. paper) |
 ISBN 9781503603820 (pbk. : alk. paper)
Subjects: LCSH: Artists--United States--Attitudes. | Artists--United
 States--Economic conditions. | Art--Economic aspects--United States.
Classification: LCC N6512.7 (ebook) | LCC N6512.7 .G47 2017 (print) |
 DDC 700.92--dc23
LC record available at https://lccn.loc.gov/2017028663

Typeset by Bruce Lundquist in 10/14 Minion Pro

To Jon and Sindre Lo. W.

Contents

Preface

What happens when art becomes work? In these pages, you will learn how visual artists make sense of the things they do, and how the stories they tell about the worth of art come together to create the boundaries of legitimate practice. Through these artists and stories, this book explores the ways that all of us talk about the things we do as worthwhile—the analogies we draw, the arguments we make, the bases of value we point to when we say: what I do is worth doing.

To write this book I spoke with a lot of artists in a lot of places, from those who show their work at MoMA and the Guggenheim to artists whose most important exhibition was at a church café in South Dakota. In 2012, I drove hundreds of miles a day through hurricane-season Louisiana and Mississippi and sweated in a gorgeous studio built by an artist there in the years after Katrina swept his life away. He threw pots while we talked, showed me his beautiful new industrial kiln, and told me about the sculpture park he envisioned for his property. Another artist told me about getting his first gun during the storm when he went down to get his mom out of New Orleans; now he mostly builds his own—semiautomatics and machine guns—but he can't take them out in public, obviously. Another artist brought me to a party and we goofed around in a photo booth; a strip of those photos is still taped today to the bookshelf in my office.

A couple of weeks earlier I had been in Los Angeles knocking at the door of a house built by an architect whose style even I recognized. The space was bare and immaculate; I took off my shoes and settled into a couch while the artist I had come to speak with, a visit that required the assistance of a powerful curator, got me a Pellegrino and poured it into a high-design glass.

The day before that I had met with a young artist at a bookstore café in a fast-gentrifying neighborhood; her hand flew to her throat unconsciously, choking, when she told me about her relationships with gallerists.

I visited a monastery in the Midwest to meet with an artist who laughed when I asked if he ran into other monks at airports, plucked at his habit, and told me that in his order they didn't always wear them. I'd arrived after driving several hours south following a day in a glassblower's studio, and my face was still red, burned by his enormous furnaces. I went to an elementary school in a tiny town consisting mainly of a senior center with WWII and Korean War uniforms in the window. It was filled with elderly folks playing bingo and talking loudly, and a hand-lettered sign in the window read "Freedom isn't free." At the school I watched as an artist patiently taught children to finger-knit, her daughter and husband in tow. We left at lunchtime to eat together at a small diner full of road crew workers in bright vests. Their daughter made tiny origami animals from our napkin bands.

This book is about how artists make the things they do worth doing, and about the ways they mold the boundaries of the art field when they do. In these pages, you will see how disagreements about value can reshape those boundaries, and find out how artists balance "doing it for love" with "doing it for money." And I'll show how, and why, all this talk about value matters so much.

.   .   .

In writing this book I have been lucky to have had the support of a remarkable intellectual community and an even more amazing group of family and friends. While there are many more of you than are acknowledged by name here, I hope you know who you are. Thank you all.

This book is most especially for and thanks to Jon Eriksen and Sindre Lo Gerber. Thank you both.

To Allen and Kathy Gerber, Andrew Gerber, and Ardie Gerber; to Janice Purvis, Don Mabley-Allen, Ben Krikava, John Knuth, Joseph del Pesco, and Helena Keeffe; to Erik Sandelin, Åsa Ståhl, Andreas Kurtsson, Jenny Nordberg, Kristina Lindström, Nicklas Marelius, and Andrei Siclodi; to Tony Barnes, Meghan Brennan, Macke Maddox, Nicol McCoy Maddox, Keren Kurti, Clara Rutenbeck, Lucy Joske, Mary Larew, and Rachel Felson; to Joseph

Klett, Clayton Childress, Sorcha Brophy, Anna Lund, Stefan Lund, Matt Norton, Johannes Lang, Matthias Revers, Mike Degani, Erik Hannerz, Sam Stabler, Shai Dromi, Elizabeth Breese, Sam Southgate, Thomas Franssen, Lise Soskolne, Matt Lawrence, Jane Halpern, April Britski, and Carrie Schneider; to Dominic Power, Johan Jansson, Rhiannon Pugh, Taylor Brydges, Patrik Aspers and Stefan Jonsson; to Yale University, the Bergman Foundation, and Kerstin Kalström; to Ben Snyder, Francesca Tripodi, Ryann Manning, Roscoe Scarborough, Julia Ticona, Angèle Christin, and Ryan Hagen; to Stanford University Press, Kate Wahl, Jenny Gavacs, Micah O'Brien Siegel, and four anonymous reviewers; to Ron Eyerman and Jim Scott, and very especially to Rene Almeling, Frederick Wherry, Amy Wrzesniewski, and Julia Adams; to everyone, thank you.

THE WORK OF ART

Art Work?

WHEN I FIRST MET THE ARTIST WILLIAM SCHAFF I paid $80 to do it. Will wears homemade masks in photographs, and for years I had no idea what he looked like. I just knew his work: a papercut and a few lithographs framed on my walls, the cover of a favorite album. But in 2014, Will went to the internet with a plea for help. As a self-employed artist, his income wasn't steady, and he had fallen behind. He was losing his home, a small building that houses his studio and a few other artists' apartments and serves as an ad hoc community center. He made a short video and set up a fundraiser on a crowdfunding website, dubbing it "Hold Down the Fort!" The crowdfunding model encourages offering rewards to funders, and Will's rewards were a mix of existing artworks, new works, services, tokens, and promises. A $9 donation got you a deck of playing cards designed by Will, $30 a small print. For $50, he would paint a small banner with your name on the wall of the Fort. For $200, he would spend an hour speaking to you on a webcam, without a mask. For $360, he would send you handmade, unique mail art each month for a year. And, of course, for $80: "spend a day at the Fort. I can give you art lessons, or we can just create things together but the point is, it is your day. From 9 am to 4 pm." It was such a strange offer—with such a strange "price"—that I had to take him up on it. I put the money on a credit card and signed up for a day in Will's studio; over the course of the fundraiser, nineteen others did the same. In a month, the online campaign raised $47,812 to save Fort Foreclosure.

A few months later I made it to Rhode Island to spend that day in the studio with Will. I tiptoed around a broken screen door into a room full of drawings, paintings, toys, taxidermy, tools, everything. A huge desk stood in the corner of that front room, covered with papers, cups filled with pens, small boxes, files, computers. A bearded man with close-cropped hair stood behind it, smoking. He called out, Hello! Miss Alison?

We pulled out some chairs and drinks and we talked. Will had always been good at drawing, he said; it was a way to be with people, to get attention. He pulled out a picture he had made as a small child: a pen drawing of a baseball player, his dad's favorite baseball player, getting hit on the head with a ball. His father had put it in a little acrylic document frame. The paper had stuck out a bit on three edges and now it was a little frayed and dirty. When his father died a few years ago, Will brought it home.

When Will went to art school, he thought he was going to be an illustrator. He had been really good, had won awards. But partway through his degree he hit the wall with an illustration for an article about pop-country star Garth Brooks. His teachers had really liked it, and they were holding it up and talking about it to the other students, and he realized: I don't want my name to be associated with that. Will switched to the fine arts track, but he brought design and illustration skills along with him. For a while, for work, he used to design figurines for a Chinese company that made Christmas village scenes. For years. He would draw an idea, a front view, and if the company liked it he would draw the back view, and sometimes they would buy the design. He pulled out a binder and paged through it, showing me those old designs. Children throwing snowballs; you always just put a wreath or a puppy in there, and they'll buy it, that's what he learned. He told me that his mom had all of the figurines he had designed, that she was really proud of him. Over the years it got to be tough, though, and he would put all these little jokes in there. The last one he did was supposed to be a Christmas bazaar scene. And he did it, but all the shopkeepers' tables were set up like the Last Supper. And he spelled bazaar "bizarre." And the company said, thanks, but no thanks. One time he was delivering pizzas, back when the standard tip was fifty cents. And when one woman opened the door, he saw she had the entire village set up, all the stuff he had designed. All of it. And she was giving him the fifty-cent tip, and he was thinking, should I tell her, I designed all of that? But he didn't.

People wandered in and out of the Fort all day. Will was friendly but didn't make conversation. One man popped his head in and asked if any of the sculptures in the window were for sale. Will said no, they're part of my private collection. The man left without another word. Later, Will told me that if the guy had said, I've got $500 in my pocket, then he would have maybe said, yeah, you can have whichever one you want. He needs $500. There were only, like, two he wouldn't have let go of. But the guy led with, how much? And you know he's going to haggle. I didn't say anything about that the guy hadn't asked how much.

Will hates it when people haggle; he doesn't haggle, ever. He told me about a documentary he watched once about some artist. In it, the guy was finishing up a painting, and someone had made a deal to buy it, and they were going to pay $2000. And they came in right at the end, and said, you know, how about $1500? And the painter said, whatever, OK. And then later he had delivered the painting and the buyer called him and was, like, what the hell, man, where's the corner of the painting? And the artist was like, well, you got $1500 worth of that painting.

Late in the day, I noticed something in a huge glass case. I asked about it and Will said to feel it, pick it up. Really. Slide that glass over. He got up when I hesitated, helped me to open the case. It was a small paw and forearm, perfectly preserved. Mounted on a small, roughly hewn square of wood, a tiny pedestal. The little hand was perfect, supple, like it was alive. Will didn't know what it was: a possum? A raccoon? He told me it was made by a guy in Georgia. He was in this shop and the guy came in with a bunch of them. The shop sells them for $13 so that guy's getting $6.50 each. I said something like, that's not enough; these are amazing. Will said, well, it works out, if you use that meat for a big stew. Then it can work out.

Will doesn't have a gallerist anymore, but he has some collectors. He wouldn't be able to afford his own work now. It's tough, that. He still does some illustration work. He showed me his contract; he wrote it years ago and has used it ever since. Whenever he receives a request, he sends the contract right away so that everyone understands: there isn't going to be any back and forth. He'll talk to the client about themes and suggest a price. And you pay half up front, and half when he's done. If you don't like it, then you don't pay that second half, and both you and Will are out of luck. But in all these years there haven't been that many who weren't happy. Two, maybe. And because there's no back and forth, he still has the piece in the end, even if the client isn't happy. It's less risky. Because he's happy with what he did. He only ever really gets commissions from strangers. Album covers, tattoo designs, stationery, wedding invitations, things like that. Not for his friends—it's really hard to talk money with friends. He'd rather give it away.

We talked for a few hours, and then Will started to fidget, said he had to get to work. We talked and drew. He's got a mail art club he's had for a few years; he draws and paints on envelopes, stuffs them with ephemera, sends them to subscribers. He's had to really get efficient. He showed me images of pieces from a few years back wistfully, said look at the coloring there, look at that. That took forever. Now, he said, he tries to get them down to an hour apiece; he said he has a system. That's $30 an hour, not great, but, you know. He says he's got a system but each one I watched him make took a good bit more than an hour.

Later, we went across the street to a bar. He knew everyone there. One of his friends went back to the Fort to grab something and found a young couple wandering around inside. They'd come down from Boston to see Will's studio, were fans of his work. His friend brought them back to the bar and I felt like I should head out, leave Will to his unexpected visitors, his maybe collectors. He walked me out, and we lingered outside for a while. After a couple of minutes he said, suddenly sheepish, you know, and I tell all the folks who do this, you don't have to pay for it. I laughed and said, I know.

During my $80 trip to Will's studio, I watched him easily reject sales to the wrong people, listened to him talk about an efficiency that would have made perfect sense if he'd evidenced it in practice. His studio was a complex and enchanting world of his own making, and it was one where he had to make a living and live with himself both. Why did William offer a day at his studio for $80 when an hour with him on Skype was on offer for $200? Did he discount the day in the studio, or inflate the hour on Skype? Why $80, a sum that looked to me as though he gauged his value at $10 per hour? And why did I and so many others agree with Will about the value of the things he does—why did we offer money in exchange for physical and immaterial rewards, or (as many did) simply send gifts, when our funds are limited and so many others deserving?

.   .   .

Social studies of value have proliferated in recent years, most notably with the rise of economic sociology as a field.[1] It's not only economists who think about value; sociologists, anthropologists, psychologists, historians, political scientists, and others see questions of value as central to understanding social life. Still, economics remains dominant.[2] In that field, *value* most often translates to *price*, and models of pricing formalize valuation processes. The underlying assumptions of neoclassical economics—that individuals are rational and that they hope to maximize utility—are so powerful and intuitive that they are, today, "common knowledge." In recent decades, behavioral economics has begun to incorporate outside perspectives on price, with early work focused on explaining observed deviations from the expectations of neoclassical economics. Today, economists look to the importance of biases and systematic errors, stereotypes and heuristic reasoning, and market inefficiencies and bad information, but don't question the basic assumptions of their discipline as thoroughly as economic sociologists have.[3]

Perspectives from economics are important to this study insofar as they guide a good deal of lay theorizing about value. They drive state policy, orient tax law, tell us how to think about the value of a dollar. They almost always privilege price as the best marker of value. This study, though—which aims to make sense of both those who do and those who do not draw incomes from their work, and of a field where value is complex, ambiguous, and contentious—looks elsewhere for insight. It is situated in economic sociology, a field of inquiry where we need not assume that economic value (money) is different from, more important than, polluting of, or fatal to other forms of valuation, of other spheres of human life. An entire generation of researchers writing after Viviana Zelizer has shown, again and again, that economic life need not pit value against values. They have also shown that dollar value need not trump other forms of valuation. We price even what we claim is most priceless: human life, children, love.[4] Money, morals, and meanings mingle in the trade in human cadavers, sperm and eggs, and (literally!) hearts. The crass, blunt, mighty dollar need not supplant love, intimacy, or integrity.[5] Rather than relying on lawlike pricing models, these researchers ask what prices tell us beyond a dollar value, how emotions influence economic life, and whether market norms include reciprocity and redistribution.[6] Economic sociology departs from economics by looking closely to the actual workings of economic life as social life.

Economic judgments are often stated in terms of the common currency of . . . currency, of which there can be only more and less. Social practices can layer multiple meanings onto money, of course,[7] but at its heart, money is ordinal. We rarely aim for less money, or toward the flourishing of more diverse types of money.[8] When it comes to money, then, the goal is clear: more of it. In economic discussions, costs and benefits can be calculated and we can think rationally; above all, an ideal outcome not only exists but can be attained. Economic logic gives us something to aspire to, whereas other lenses offer less clarity. A political lens on a question, for example, might imagine two or more parties with stakes in a finite resource; we do not presume that one goal is likely to be embraced by all relevant parties. There might not be any attainable ideal outcome, nor any rational path; outcomes here have winners and losers, and the mythical, the innumerate, the nonmonetary, the communicative, and the personal hold at least as much sway as the rational.

. . .

The ideas and arguments in this book are based primarily on in-depth interviews with visual artists based in the United States. And, as I noted in the preface and discuss in more detail in the appendix, for this book I spoke with a lot of artists in a lot of places. I have carried out formal, semistructured interviews with eighty artists; all of these were recorded and then transcribed verbatim. I have tried to be careful throughout this book to refer to the "artists I spoke with," since my interactions with these artists produced the data I draw on directly, but in many instances I would be confident saying simply "artists." I have avoided doing so because my diverse sample taught me that there are many art worlds I do not know well, and because I never intend to make claims about *all* artists. But it is equally untrue to imagine that I am speaking *only* of the eighty artists represented in these pages.

Since I began this project, I have carried out participant observation in varied contexts and informal interviews with artists, curators, dealers, museum directors, art professors, art historians, viewers, and others. I have participated in countless conversations of a few moments or a few hours with artists, artists' families and friends, art world professionals, and audiences. I have been to exhibition openings, drunk bad wine, and gossiped with everyone else; I have sat in on art classes and lectures; I have hung around with museum staff and gallerists, done the things that you might expect. I don't often draw explicitly on participant observation data here, but I mention it because presenting the data considered here as "interview" data is somewhat problematic, especially in light of the assumptions often made in current debates over the merits of interview data.[9] A few of my interviews have happened in coffee shops or offices, and looked like what we might imagine when we hear the word *interview*—two speakers, interviewer and respondent, seated facing one another, a tape recorder between; at the end, a handshake. But many more of the interviews I've done have happened in people's homes and studios, have involved something more. I have stayed with interview subjects, eaten meals with them, met their partners and their children. I have cooked food for some; others have slept on my couch. Some I have spoken with once; others I am in touch with regularly; a few are now friends. All of this has served as sources of data that have contributed to this study.

Artists might seem a strange population to use to ask big questions about value—why not look at something more solid, something we really need—calories, perhaps? But artists, artworks, and artmaking are especially useful for thinking about value and valuation, for several reasons.[10] Value in the arts is openly ambiguous; there are few within or outside of art worlds who will argue that objective qualities drive pricing. Artmaking is an activity that, for something that can be a highly credentialed and well-paid profession, is also notably open to all. There are artists who paint for a living and those who spend all their money to be able to paint; artists with MFA and PhD degrees and many with no training at all. There are many other vectors of diversity in art worlds, but these two alone can be used to make a crucial point: all of these artists—the professionals and the hobbyists, the credentialed and the naïve—might be in the same exhibition, might sell their work at the same price point. Defining "quality," like "value," is a real problem in the arts.

While some researchers take art prices to be the first point of entry for the analyst interested in questions of value, I focus elsewhere. If we define artists as "people who make a living selling art objects," the resulting group of artists will include only a very small minority of those who actually produce and exhibit visual art. I am interested primarily in practices, not products, and in a plurality of artists who define goals and success in divergent ways. Whether artists turn to the markets for art objects to define the value of their activities is treated, here, as an open question.[11] But there has been very little exploration of the valuation of art *practices*, and it is on that process of valuation that I focus here. By practices I mean not only the brush-to-canvas and chisel-to-marble movements made by artists' bodies, but also artists' increasingly central discursive practices: the meaning-making and sensemaking work that can be observed in their speech and writings. Talk is just as much a part of artistic practice as the work of the hands; sometimes it's the greater portion.[12]

Because I am interested much more in the valuation of practice than in, for example, the prices of art objects or the result of an art school education, I have defined *artists* for this study through a proxy for artistic practice: the exhibition of artworks in public. (Notes on sampling and other methodological issues can be found in the appendix.) I focus especially on one window into individual artists' valuation of their own practices by looking at artists' narratives of investment and their expectations around returns on investment. I consider artists to be speaking of investments in their practice when they refer in one narrative (a story with a discernible beginning and end, of which there were many in each interview) to finite resources (for example, time, money, space, or energy) committed to their artistic practice, and *also* link such resource commitments to presumed, hoped-for, or past specific outcomes (sales, visibility, employment, the development of new skills or relationships, happiness, and so forth) of such resource commitments. The decision to narrow the scope of this study to accounts of investment was central to my analytical strategy and findings.

.   .   .

In the pages that follow, I ask how artists account for the value of the things that they do. I look for patterns in the ways artists' narratives of their own practices presume distinct bases of value, and I consider the ways that artists construct convincing accounts. I use my findings to engage with the literature on valuation and commensuration, and show why attention to disagreement is as valuable as a focus on agreement. I explain how and why the alliance of love and money is so central to contemporary artistic practice, and explore the dangers that await artists who fail to strike a balance between the two.

We should expect to see the kinds of diverse and divergent accounts of value that this book investigates in any field where a rationalized understanding of activity as valuable—as a job, an occupation—overlaps well enough with a particular collection of existing practices to largely supplant them, while fitting poorly enough to allow for friction between traditional and occupational bases of value. Stated differently, we would expect to see conflicts over value in those fields of human activity that we engaged in before economic life under capitalism made them into jobs. In such fields, we should look for patterns in the accounts of practitioners, and pay attention to the ways that diverse bases of value are used by practitioners to promote distinct strategies of valuation. Such an analysis will highlight the importance of multiple pathways to value within fields, will show how valuation and revaluation are negotiated by individuals and institutions, and will show how disparate valuations are associated with divergent outcomes.

Valuation matters, and we need a sociological perspective on it because valuation is something that we do together. We know that the value of things is not determined by their qualities or by an unseen, godlike hand. Even the "invisible hand" of Smith's market moves, like the pointer on a Ouija board, not thanks to ghostly spirits but to animal ones—we move it ourselves, together.

The Work of Art

2

WHAT MAKES ART WORTH DOING, and how does that change when long-established art practices evolve into something that looks more like a modern job? In recent decades, artistic practice has undergone a sort of occupational turn, with artists today experiencing their practices as "serious" "work," a "job," a "profession"—this despite the minority of artists who make a living at art work. But this is a *new* normal; as recently as 1969, artists claiming to speak on behalf of their colleagues could still insist that "artists are not workers, because all persons who regard themselves as artists are artists, no matter what their activities."[1] Yet, over time, those who regarded themselves as artists and also argued that they should be understood as workers enjoyed increasing visibility in the art community, while many of those dissenting absented themselves from the discussion. Consider Lee Lozano: in 1969, she held the line against an encroaching occupational art world, writing, "I will not call myself an art worker but rather an art dreamer."[2] That year she publicly performed a withdrawal from the art world with *General Strike Piece* and, in 1972, she dropped out entirely.[3] As this chapter will show, the art workers have won, and the past fifty years have seen a thorough reconceptualization of artistic activity. Today, artists declare simply, "Art-making is labor. Art-making is my job."[4] Making art has become work.

This chapter considers the occupational turn in artistic practice, a rapid cultural change that set the stage for the contemporary artists that are the focus of this book. To illuminate this transformation and its effects, I will split my discussion of artists' narratives of themselves as workers and arguments about the value of their work into two eras—the 1960s through the 1970s and the 1980s to the present—with a short aside between the two sections to consider the ways that stable terminology can mask changing meanings. The occupational turn has had important effects on artistic practice, most obviously around artists' understandings of the value of the things that they do and the appropriate ways to ask for remuneration. In the 1960s and 70s, artists imagined themselves as primarily producers of objects: they argued that their labor was worthy of remuneration because they had *made things*. But beginning in the 1980s artists began to think of themselves in a new way, and today they are much more likely to say that their labor is worthy of remuneration because they have *done things*.

When a set of practices turns into a job, it undergoes change; professionalization processes drive and reflect still greater changes. Professional work is unlikely to look or feel much like traditional practice, even when the tasks required remain the same.[5] Artmaking is a lot like the other things that we have done since we crawled from the sea and that life under capitalism has turned only partly, haltingly, into jobs.

Consider for a moment a comparison between artmaking and the care of young children. We have always made things that look today like what we call art; similarly, we have always cared for children and others who needed it. Today, caring for children is work that can be done for free or for very high pay; you can learn to do it by acquiring advanced degrees or you can jump in headfirst. Some people care for their own kin; others exclusively for others' children. There are innumerable visions of what "quality" child care looks like, and even more ideas about how to achieve it. Sometimes it's worth a lot in dollar terms, sometimes very little; sometimes it's done for love, sometimes for money—just like so many other things that have undergone a contested and partial transformation with our move to money economies and the need for cash income.[6]

Artists, like many others, commit to something that is not unambiguously worth their time. Traditional practice, occupational practice, and professional practice overlap in meaningful ways, to be sure, but differences are everywhere, and our impulse is to see meaning in variation, to amplify even minor distinctions and find substance in them.[7] These differences allow for many points of conflict, and these conflicts, together with the opportunities they generate, are key to understanding how artists make sense of art as worth doing.

.   .   .

Artistic practices—the production of "artworks" as well as other forms of creative practice, like the things we call decorative and folk arts—have always had nonmarket value (especially evident in the private sphere) as well as market value. Historically, a wide variety of individuals have engaged in art work, from those who learned their craft at home and worked exclusively in household production to "fine" artists who pursued long apprenticeships, copying the work of their masters until their reproductions were gauged appropriately authentic. Some artists and artisans have always been able to make a living through commissioned work, patronage, or sales. But while the apprenticeship model and, later, the academy model gathered strength by the nineteenth century, those who hoped to make a living as artists still followed no set path. Well into the twentieth century the notion of artistic practice as a "job" was rare, though many understood what they did as work and of course some made a living at it.[8] The occupational turn I discuss below is not a shift from autonomous and private practice to market work. Artists have engaged with the market in ways that mirror some contemporary practices for centuries. This is, rather, a story of rationalization: of increasing numbers of artists making sense of their practice as a modern job.

   The majority of this book is based on research with artists in the United States, but to look back we must begin by looking further afield to Europe, the birthplace of much of the American artistic tradition and a training ground for early American artists. There, high artmaking was for hundreds of years a more or less straightforward trade—the "picture trade," employing artisans, master craftsmen, in contractual relationships with men we now remember as "patrons."[9] In his study of fifteenth-century Italy, art historian Michael Baxandall shows us the folly of thinking of those relationships in such terms: he writes that the Renaissance artist made artworks for an "active, determining and not necessarily benevolent agent in the transaction of which the painting is the result: we can fairly call him a client. The better sort of fifteenth century painting was made on a bespoke basis, the client asking for a manufacture after his own specifications."[10] During the Renaissance, a period thought by many to represent a high-water mark in painting and sculpture, artists' contracts reached remarkable levels of sophistication along with their command of color and line. The specifics of subject matter, size, pigment, time to delivery, and framing were regularly negotiated and laid out in detail between artists and their clients. Artists rarely followed the muse, instead adhering to their contractual obligations like any other businessperson, despite the slow rise of a distinction between art and craft and an emphasis on individual artistry.[11]

Letters from the time and up through the Baroque period between artists and their clients often highlight the level of control clients had over artists' work; they also offer insight into the ways that artists aimed to increase their profit margins, and show how easily artists spoke of commerce.[12] Witness, for example, Benozzo Gozzoli's attempt to defend his aesthetic choices even as he bows to the wishes of one of the Medicis in 1459. He writes, "This morning I received a letter from Your Magnificence, by the hand of Roberto Martelli. From which it appears that you do not find that the cherubim I have painted are suitable." He claims that the cherubim in question are trivial: "One of these I have set in a corner, among clouds, of which only the tips of the wings are visible; and he is so much concealed, and the clouds cover him in such manner, that he causes no uncomeliness, but rather gives beauty." He argues that the client's intermediary, Martelli, agrees: "Martelli saw them, and declared that the thing was of no consequence." But in the end, Gozzoli bows to his client's wishes, writing, "I will do as you shall command; two clouds will quickly dispose of them."[13]

The great Peter Paul Rubens, remembered today for his sensual renderings of human flesh, grovels in a letter to a displeased client in 1621 after being caught cutting corners by farming too much work out to his studio assistants. "I am quite willing that the picture painted for My Lord Ambassador Carleton be returned to me and that I should paint another hunting piece less terrible than that of the lions, making rebate as is reasonable for the amount already paid." His next words guarantee no more shortcuts: "the new picture to be entirely by my own hand without admixture of the work of anyone else, which on the word of a gentleman I will carry out." He apologizes, but at the letter's end can't help but try to deflect blame, arguing that the client should have been more careful when the two wrote their contract: "I am very sorry that there should have been any dissatisfaction on the part of Mr. Carleton, but he would never give me to understand clearly, though I often entreated him to do so, whether this picture was to be entirely original or merely touched by my own hand."[14] One last example, a rather delightful note from Albrecht Dürer to a client, written in 1509, shows just how comfortable artists of the time were with frank wheeling and dealing. Dürer writes, "I am happy to learn that my picture pleases you, so that the pains I took over it were not in vain. I am glad, too, that you are content with the price—as is right, for I might have received 100 guilders more for it than you gave me, but I would not; I left it to you, for I hope thus to continue in your friendship."[15]

Real changes were under way even as this no-bones-about-it approach to artmaking reigned; while artmakers prior to the 1400s nearly always produced anonymously,[16] their craft holding little special status, the Renaissance saw the slow birth of the "artist" as we know them today. Some artists gained salaried employment in royal courts, allowing them exemption from guild membership and a sense of personal irreplaceability. Skill grew, over the years, to be understood and valued in new ways, and the first academies of the arts were founded. By the time the bourgeois began to collect artworks, allowing artists to create commodities for purchase rather than filling custom orders, the notion of the individualized artist-as-creator was widespread. As early as the 1600s in the Netherlands, artists were working with dealers and producing work on an open market. Over time, across Europe, the atelier-workshop model grew less common, with the growth of the academy and professional roles for artist-teachers expanded. Artists' status rose, along with their individuality, and the market for art grew beyond state and religious clients.[17]

But what about the garret painter of the past? As a rejection of rationalism, didacticism, censorship, and the instrumentalization of artistic practice, the rallying cry of "art for art's sake" first emerged in the early nineteenth century.[18] It was both aesthetic and economic in its aims: art needed no justification, the argument went, and artists should both recognize and follow their muse. This new attitude was enabled by a burgeoning system of small private galleries; by 1850, it was widespread along with notions of the artist as special, different, and unique that have dominated our ideas of artists and their work ever since.[19] But, of course, there were always some who refused the romantic, bohemian pose, and by the early 1900s they found ammunition in the writings of Marx and new models in socialist political tactics.

During the period between the First and Second World Wars, socialist-influenced artists' groups coalesced around ideas about artists as workers and the explicit rejection of art-for-art's-sake thinking.[20] Artists' groups in the United States, building on small-scale successes in the early 1930s, successfully pushed for the development and funding of the Federal Art Project in 1935. This involved recasting artists—who before (and for the most part, since) had simply gotten by as best they could, often by working in "day jobs" and professional careers not associated with the arts—as "unemployed artists." By achieving this designation, artists made themselves just as worthy of relief as other unemployed workers hit by the Great Depression. Ten thousand artists, artisans, craftspeople, and others were employed through the Art Project and the other three New Deal art schemes; they were paid the highest wages allowable under the Works Progress Administration and exempted from the strict eligibility requirements demanded of other kinds of workers.[21] While most artists who participated in the Art Project were arguably better off economically during the Depression than they had been before the crisis began, the money didn't come without strings: artists had to work more or less to spec, and many did not do their "own work" at all but taught children or the unemployed or worked in administrative jobs. Though "easel painters" were free to work at home, in New York City they had to head downtown to punch a clock early in the morning and at the end of the day, with the required commute sometimes taking up the bulk of their "working" day.[22] Jobs, even for artists, came with employers' expectations. Still, the Great Depression is remembered by many as a golden era of artistic practice in the United States, a time when more artists than ever before could live off their art.

The experience of the 1930s changed the meaning of art practice in the United States. Artists—a diverse and incoherent group, compared to generations before—came together and agitated for themselves as members of a class deserving of rights. Across the country, in rural areas as in cities,

Americans were made aware of artists in their midst, and the fruits of those artists' labor were made public. Many artists had the experience of being paid a relatively high salary for their efforts, one befitting a professional. A version of the artist's identity that still prevails today was born, one based in a primary commitment to artistic practice. Willem de Kooning, employed for just one year by the Art Project, summarized how the experience had changed him: "I changed my attitude toward being an artist. Instead of doing odd jobs and painting on the side, I painted and did odd jobs on the side. My life was the same, but I had a different view of it."[23] By the end of the Art Project, artists in the United States were (at least potentially) workers. They had seen previously unimaginable models for artistic practice and remuneration function, if temporarily, and the groundwork had been laid for much broader changes beginning in the late 1960s that would change artists into art workers and transform art into a job.

.   .   .

Art historian Julia Bryan-Wilson traces the emergence of the "art worker" to the 1960s in the United States. While she focuses on aesthetic change, she also argues that the identity of the art worker was necessary for artists to claim a stable social position and a platform from which to assert political identities.[24] In the 1960s and '70s, the desire to be seen as an art worker was visible but not yet universal, even in the high art worlds Bryan-Wilson describes: recall Lee Lozano, the "art dreamer"; she was not the only one.[25] The rationalization of artistic practice was under way but had not yet been widely embraced. Over the next fifty years, though, changes in the ways that artists thought about the production and sale of art objects, the value of their time, and the appropriate attitude toward art work would take hold across art worlds; art was well on its way to becoming a job.

To understand the ways that art has become work, it will be useful, again, to look to a transnational art world rather than restricting ourselves to the American case. Artistic practice has for decades been globalized and has included, for many elites at least, a good deal of travel and international exchange. Ideas and individuals move easily across national borders and bring with them new visions of the role of the artist and the value of artmaking. Below, I look artists in the US and in two other countries selected to reflect diverse approaches to artistic support: Canada, with its social insurance system and an increasingly well-developed standardized artists' fee system, and Sweden, a social democratic welfare state with far-reaching state support for the arts.[26] There are real differences between the experiences of practicing artists in these three countries, but on the issues considered here there is also remarkable similarity; differences concern local strategies rather than divergent meanings.[27]

Artists have always made and sold objects, and those activities were at the heart of making a living as an artist in the 1960s and '70s as in the centuries before. In interviews with artists from the '60s and '70s, remarkably little time is spent on the specifics and meaning of artist-dealer relationships, prices, or other features of making a living selling art. When the topic is discussed, it is almost always in a perfunctory fashion, as it is already understood, by interviewers and artists alike, that there is one path to a career in the arts: the production and sale of objects, preferably through a prestigious gallery and at a healthy but not exorbitant profit.[28] But object-making moves from discursively central to discursively embarrassing over the following decades.

The sale of objects could be taken for granted by artists speaking in the 1960s and '70s, given that there were few other options for artists to draw an income from their work. Consider the straightforward market orientation of Emma Amos, speaking in 1968: "The thing that influences my work most is what am I going to do with it." She clarifies, "If you have no outlet to sell it then sort of what's the point in doing it?" She says that the checks coming in "from this being sold or that being sold" are pure motivation: "It makes me feel good and it pushes me on to doing more work."[29]

While artists in the 1960s and '70s often positioned themselves as "art workers," unlike many other workers they most often had no employer when it came to their art practice; they were entrepreneurs, and as such needed to show the world the value of the things that they did, had to negotiate that value with others, and had to find ways to exploit systems built for others to get paid. At that time, artists most often argued that the value resulting from their work resided in the multiple uses of the products that they created and distributed. The job, as it was imagined, was one where artists make things that have value. Artists' core tasks involved production and distribution, and artists came together in associations and organizations to promote the value of those core tasks. In 1967, a Canadian artist wrote that "the painting or sculpture etc. is a MATERIA PRIMA, the raw product from which many business concerns derive profit." He pointed to a sense then rumbling through art communities far and wide: "The artist should be the first to benefit from his own work in this process but in fact, he has no place in the present arrangement."[30]

Artists' writings from that time in the United States demand that "the museum, collector or publication would compensate the artist for use of his art."[31] In a 1973 newsletter, a group of artists in Canada describe the aims of an organization they are trying to start: "to uncover the means, implicit in the works themselves, for providing revenue to the practicing artist . . . there are various means of recovering income inherent in the works themselves."[32] This letter continues with a call for exhibition fees, colloquially referred to here and elsewhere as "rental fees."[33] Artists, secure in the belief that the value they produced lay in their objects, argued primarily for better copyright provisions, and they fought hard for both reproduction and exhibition royalties.

Artists of that time conceptualized their practice as being based in the provision of objects for use, objects that consisted of both physical and intellectual property. Copyright provisions were seen as the key both to artists' control over their own work and to reimbursement for their efforts, and enforcement of existing copyright law and expansion of that law were seen by the vast majority as appropriate goals. Demands were made in two arenas in particular: artists demanded control over reproductions of their work (royalty payments) as well as rental fees when their works were shown, whether or not those works had been sold. The demand for control over reproductions was, relatively speaking, straightforward: in most cases, it involved only enforcement of existing law. In 1969, an American artist suggested that artworks were primarily intellectual property: he argued that artworks were like manuscripts for popular novels; after purchasing the work, "the owner can keep it, or show it to his friends, but the artist continues to hold the rights of reproduction, including the right to collect royalties if he wants them."[34] The argument for rental fees was seen as an extension of the logics behind reproduction royalties, and terms like *royalties, rental fees,*

and *exhibition fees* were interchangeable. Another artist clarified that, as artworks were both physical and intellectual properties, artists should be compensated for their use even after sale: "this is a rental, beyond the original
purchase price . . . the principle of a royalty would be used."[35] That artist, like
many others, hoped that even after the sale of an artwork, the artist would
be entitled to some measure of control over the artwork and payment for its
use.[36] These views were widespread in a rapidly globalizing and interconnected art world. Across the Atlantic, in 1971, a Swedish artist argued simply,
in a speech during a union demonstration, that "the artist should be given
an exhibition fee for the right to use the work."[37] Another artist, ten years
later and after significant changes in that union's leadership, continued the
same line, saying that "full payment for constant access to the fruits of our
labor" was both legitimate and necessary.[38]

This argument developed over several decades and is still instrumentalized by artists in efforts to enforce copyright law, create new copyright
provisions, and obtain royalties and resale rights. Well into the 1980s, artists
were still regularly explaining to other artists that the work they did was the
creation of objects that had value. In a newsletter article titled "Copyright—
the Profitable Practice of Protecting Your Right," a Canadian artist explains
copyright law in simple terms, speaking to colleagues as explicitly as possible: "When an artist creates an original work of art, s/he really creates two
separate and distinct pieces of property. One is the work of art itself, which
the artist may sell, trade or otherwise dispose of as desired. The second
property is the copyright, or right to reproduce the work of art." He continues his lecture: "Stop thinking of copyright as valueless and unimportant.
Make it a commodity separate from the work itself in your own mind, then
treat it with the care and consideration that you would give any valuable
property that you own."[39] Such explanations were necessary and in demand
as part of artists' professional education.

Artists did recognize some of the limitations of reliance on copyright and
of defining their work in terms of intellectual and physical property, but for
many years stuck with the logic. In 1978 in Canada, a legal brief argued that
"by temperament, logic, and product, the visual artist shares few, if any of the
protective adaptations either in custom or legislation available to the author
or composer," later suggesting that "the original of a work of art occupies a

special position which has no equivalent in other fields of artistic or literary creation." At the time, copyright issues were central; the solution proposed by these authors, then, was "special and individual consideration in the reform of copyright law."[40] Artists were secure in their position as object-makers; so secure, in fact, that the language and theory of property rights was the only one that made real sense. Property rights could and should be twisted, contorted, and extended: because the basis of the value of artistic practice was in the provision of objects, protecting artists' rights over those objects was clearly the best way to achieve artists' goals of remuneration and recognition.

.   .   .

Just a few decades later, the value of artistic practice is now understood in very different terms, and new solutions are possible. Ten years ago, a Canadian artist pointed to the problem that that copyright theorists couldn't solve: that "[rental] fees are meant to partially compensate for the time and cost of the production of the actual artworks. Artists are not compensated for the preparation costs."[41] A real shift was underway; artists, who had long argued that their core tasks revolved around the objects they produced, began slowly to view themselves as hourly workers, providing as-yet-unacknowledged services.[42]

This term, *services*, deserves special attention here. A look at a single long-running artists' organization, Canadian Artists' Representation (CAR, later CARFAC), indicates that even within a single group and single national context, the meaning of services shifted in important ways between the 1970s and the present, despite real gains that should have served to solidify old ways of thinking. Throughout the 1970s, members of CAR argued that their basic principle was "fair exchange," a principle they further described as "payment for services" that they instrumentalized, rationalized, and advocated for as rental fees; the "service" they provided was the provision of objects for rental. An example of such an argument, written by a CAR founder, reads: "The fair-exchange principle is one which society already acknowledges for its multitude of dealings, and is simply understood as payment for services. Everyone performing a service in our society is paid in return." He raised the stakes: "The cultural basis for society is created by artists; and we are agreeing with the rest of organized society that services do in fact require payment. Hence our suggested fee schedule."[43] The "fee schedule" here is, of course, an outline of recommended rental fees for the provision of objects; "professional services" were not added to the fee schedule for another ten years.

Throughout the 1980s and 1990s, CAR remained concerned with artists' rights as the creators and owners of intellectual property. But as early as 1983, the first suggestions that artists' time might have value are visible; an artist wrote then, in a comment on a new federal cultural policy document, "Visual artists will not be surprised to learn that 'the largest subsidy to the cultural life of Canada comes not from government, corporations or other patrons, but from the artists themselves, through their unpaid or underpaid labour,'"[44] The issue of artists' labor appeared irregularly and almost always in direct connection with the production of objects in CAR's newsletters and meeting minutes from 1968 forward, and then, in 2005, an editorial appeared in the group's newsletter, strongly arguing for a notion of "services" that valued artists' time as well as their products.

An argument that was hardly thinkable in the 1970s was, rather suddenly, entirely rational and appropriate. The author calculated the hours he generally spent on such tasks as correspondence with galleries and shipping work, and estimated that, outside of the time taken to produce artworks themselves, he spent about sixty hours preparing for a large exhibition. He polled a variety of artists, who pointed out ways that he had lowballed his estimate, and then settled on an average of 100 hours labor for each exhibition—again, his estimate presumes a body of completed work, ready for installation.[45] He did not argue that the time spent making the artwork (thinking, looking, making) should be included in this estimate, and in leaving it out he takes one side in what today is a central conflict among those who advocate for the value of artists' time: whether or not the time an artist spends making art has value, what sort of value that might be, and whether and how to pursue remuneration. But this artist's strategy—to focus on administrative and logistical tasks done directly in service of an organization, to the exclusion of the majority of the tasks of artmaking—is today common. Extant fees in this context (rental fees) as well as, presumably, sales, are understood by this author to "cover" artmaking time but not the time spent preparing for exhibitions, work now conceptualized as a form of service.

   Members of CAR have made significant concrete gains over the decades. Among other things, they succeeded in pushing for changes to national copyright provisions that should have served to ensconce 1970s thinking in an institutional framework, strengthening artists' identities as the producers of objects and increasing incentives for artists to produce works that could be protected by copyright and to think of themselves as primarily producers of intellectual property. But even within this organizational and national context, members came to argue that the service artists provided was no longer the provision of objects for purchase or rental. The service provided by artists today includes their time, the hours they spend in service to institutions that they consider employers.

   CAR is a useful site for looking at a long-running conversation about artists' remuneration, but examples of these shifts abound in other contexts as well. In Sweden in the early 1970s, artists' "cultural contribution" was understood as the production of exhibitions. Artists argued explicitly that the primary service artists provided was the production of exhibitions, and that fair pay should come via the objects that artists made and maintained intellectual property rights over.[46] But by 2000, artists there were arguing that their practice had gone "from being primarily oriented toward the production of products to, to a much greater extent, being about skills, experiences, and other processes."[47] In 2004, an artist wrote a long debate article on the difference between rental fees and other forms of payment, arguing that the rental principle was not appropriate: that "what artists expect and demand payment for is their efforts, their labor," and suggested that a contract based in labor law (not copyright) regulating hourly payments was appropriate "when artists produce exhibitions on assignment."[48] And back in the United States, an artist wrote in 1997 that "all artistic work, or labor, that is not compensated through the sale of a tangible product must be considered a form of service provision."[49] That text is today widely reproduced and well-known, and its author sits on the board of an artists' organization devoted to "establishing a sustainable labor relation between artists and the institutions that contract them."[50]

                              .   .   .

Recall Emma Amos, and her comfortable orientation to a sales market. Today, selling objects requires, for many artists, an excuse, an explanation, and a specific relationship to capitalism and value. Look at the tortured contortions of another artist, Franco Mondini-Ruiz. Speaking in 2004, he felt the need to justify his sale of objects: while the production and sale of objects is still central to the practices of most working artists, it has been demoted morally. He began by talking about elite galleries, including his own, saying, "They want prestige and a good reputation, and it's a game. It's all an illusion." He said he was both "attracted and repulsed at the artificiality and the elitism of it," and then admitted: "I'm part of the snobbery game because I'm an object-maker and I make knick-knacks for the rich." Discomfort with his situation led to a new strategy, selling paintings himself, on the street, for $99 each. "As far as making a living on art, I want to do it in a more socialist way and this is going to be my formula. I might lose my gallery. But right now, she [his gallerist] is going to allow me to do a four-day show in New York. She is embarrassed about it." He explained his aim: "I want to just have this business that—it's very democratic and I make work that's very affordable, and worth my while and makes people happy, and I don't have to depend on the white elite to give my life meaning, you know?" He loved making those paintings and selling them cheaply. Still, selling has a tinge of filthy lucre, and he claimed that it was the particularities of his past that explained his comfort with sales. He grew up working-class and then middle-class with parents who owned a few electronics stores: "Don't forget I come from—we are peddlers, you know, and I love selling things." Later, when asked about sales, he reached back to his heritage again to excuse his comfort with the market, explaining, "I got that from my mother, a kind of a gypsy way of wanting—loving the cash, just loving the cash, touching it and counting it. I didn't even know what I wanted to do with it."[51]

Today there are many pathways to a remunerative life in the arts, and significant inequalities in the art world mean that one cannot assume much about those who report a relationship with a gallery.[52] The production and sale of objects is no longer the default way to make a living. It is still a pathway to a career in the arts, but now a highly visible one, a sort of boardwalk hovering over the landscape that requires a bit of buttressing for those who follow the walk's narrow path, with its pitfalls and rotted planks.

Artists were once object-makers focused on property rights; today, artists making those same kinds of objects look instead to those objects' travels through institutional spaces—the service the artists provide—when they demand remuneration for their activities. The idea that artists produce exhibitions "on assignment" in service of institutions that request them has now spread widely; artists today use it to point out that they ask not for some kind of citizen's wage but, rather, ask simply for payment when their services are in demand by others. Attention to the changing meaning of the word services shows clearly how radically artists have reconceptualized the core, value, and tasks of their practice, even as the words they used remained stable. It has become reasonable for artists to see value in their time and to think of themselves, especially when it comes to asking to be paid, as primarily service providers and only secondarily producers of objects. Artists today are likely to argue that their time, and in particular the provision of services to clients who have requested them, is the element of their practice that has value. An American artist, speaking from a podium at the Park Avenue Armory in 2008, explained why she demands payment for her time, and like others she framed her demands as rational: "We're not asking for the world, we are asking simply to be paid for our labor." The crowd applauded; a woman at the front shouted, simply and flatly, "Yes." The artist continued, providing evidence: "Museums want performance art for free? What do they think? That we dream it up while we are watching TV during the commercials? That's work. That's days, or weeks or months of work." She called on institutions to recognize artists' work, to recognize that "what is making their cultural institution 'rich' is the product of months or years of unpaid labor,"[53] and to pay artists for that labor directly.

Artists today very rarely suggest that they have any special status, preferring instead to emphasize contributions to institutions that request their services, as, in the past, they focused on institutions that requested their products. Making an argument I have heard repeated everywhere my fieldwork has brought me, a group of Swedish artists wrote in a 2006 editorial: "Though we have the greatest role among all who work with exhibitions, our work is still not paid." This group, in a common refrain, pointed to the institution: "Everyone else—directors, curators, technicians, guards, art handlers—who is a part of the work of an exhibition sees it as obvious that they should be paid for their work. Why is our work not valued in the same way?"[54] The "work" discussed here, again, is that involved in mounting one exhibition; the activities involved in making the artworks themselves are understood to be remunerated separately. In another editorial, written in 2007, the same group assigned a dollar value per hour to artists' labor and calculated the "subsidy" artists give to the state in the form of work on exhibitions, following in the footsteps of the Canadian artist discussed above. Here, pointing to exhibitions at municipal galleries, they claim that artists "carry out unpaid work for the state and local governments worth 300 million crowns per year";[55] their work "is in demand, but is not remunerated in proportion to the work carried out."[56] When artistic practice as work is visualized as hourly labor on behalf of presenting institutions, artists ask not for copyright protections or resale rights but hourly pay, taxed and otherwise treated the same as other workers' wages and salaries. They are simply, as three American artists write, "asking to be factored into our own equation, paid fees for honest work, to be equal participants in the economy."[57]

Artists' practices have changed relatively little over the past fifty years, and the language they have used to make claims about themselves as workers has remained largely stable as well. Artists spoke then as today of the value of their "services," their "work." Close attention to artists' claims, however, shows that their sense of themselves as workers, and particularly the way that they promote the value of their efforts, has changed in meaningful ways over the past fifty years. These valuations have been instrumental in the evolving discussion of the value of art work as well in changes to artists' sense of themselves as workers.

Artistic practice today has undergone an occupational turn, with artists generally required to present themselves as "full-time," "working" artists or risk the loss of diverse benefits as well as social standing within the field, no matter their source of income.[58] Almost all of the artists I spoke with called themselves "serious" or "professional" artists. Few of the artists I spoke with ever referred to themselves as hobbyists or amateurs; none under the age of forty did. Many explicitly differentiated themselves from "hobby" and "amateur" artists, nearly spitting at the words. For example, Amy[59] told me, "I have a mortgage, I have a kid. I can't have a *hobby*."[60]

. . .

The requirement of the occupationally committed pose, along with a low bar for entry, means that while art after the occupational turn is highly rationalized and seen by most as a "job," the notoriously low chances of economic success in the winner-take-all economy of the arts do not lead to fewer practitioners entering the field.[61] Rather, the "working artist" identity is available to a broader and more diverse group than ever before, including many who—when artistic practice was "serious" only when you made a living at it—had no public life as "artists" before. While the upper echelons of the high art world and the monetary rewards to be found there are still exclusive to a disappointing degree,[62] the arts in general are remarkably open, and today, varied art worlds provide supportive, challenging, and sometimes remunerative platforms for a rich diversity of artists.

The occupational turn of the past fifty years is complete: in today's art worlds, anything resembling serious participation or a hope that one might contribute to "the conversation" tends to require the performance of occupational commitment. If the occupational turn has changed artistic practice and its meanings over the past fifty years, a professionalization of the field (many elements of which can already be seen across art worlds) may be next.

What would professionalization look like in the arts? Art historian Howard Singerman points to the growth of university-based professional schools as crucial to the development of artists' professional identity, and with that growth the decline of sales as the singular path through which artists may receive compensation for their work.[63] Today, increasing numbers of visual artists attend degree-granting programs at the bachelor's level, attend such programs in university settings rather than independent art schools, and obtain master of fine arts degrees.[64] As late as the 1960s and '70s, artists who attended independent art academies were not guaranteed any kind of academic degree,[65] and relatively few attended master's or PhD degree programs in arts practice. Today, art students are nearly always granted college credit and associate's, bachelor's, or master's degrees, and most universities provide degrees in the fine arts at at least the bachelor's level.[66] As MFA programs became the norm, art as a profession has developed in new directions. The increased necessity of the MFA has promoted an expansion of opportunities for full-time professional work as an artist, including but not limited

to increased opportunities for college teaching.[67] New skills—especially
discursive skills and related writing and rhetorical practices—have become
central to the practice of art.

In high-status art worlds, a professional bearing is fast becoming the
only appropriate stance.[68] If we look to the literature on professionalization,
we can glimpse a possible future. If the professional project continues in
the art world, we might expect to see the development of strong artists' associations with control over important resources, an increased emphasis on
narrowly defined training and qualifications and theoretical knowledge, and
occupational closure to keep "amateurs" and other outsiders from practicing or being recognized for their efforts. Those elites that survive the process
may tend up better off, enjoying more autonomy and authority; the breadth
and diversity American art worlds exhibit will almost certainly be dimin-
ished.[69] At the moment, though (however central it may feel in some communities), professionalization is still nascent, and given the lack of strong,
united organizational actors, the project of professionalization may not succeed in the United States in the near future.

                              .   .   .

The Renaissance painter obediently covering a cherub that has displeased
his client is, it is clear, meaningfully different from the Impressionist living
poorly off family wealth in a garret and following his muse, painting for art's
sake three hundred years later. Neither would likely have thought much of
the New Deal painter submitting an unsigned representational canvas every
four weeks to the government; they probably would have lost all respect on
finding that those paintings were destined to be discarded—burned—like
scrap, since they were just make-work for a generation of painters who successfully argued that they were unemployed, but not that their products had
any real value.[70] None of these artists of the past would have found it easy to
fall into step with the artists of the 1960s and 70s who argued for intellectual
property protections, and even fewer would have recognized the vision of
artistic practice set forward today by those who call for recognition of their
services to institutions and hope to one day land a tenured teaching position.

These divergent visions of art practice—of the appropriate role, stance,
and identity of the artist; of proper relationships between artists and their

patrons, commissioners, families, employers, and the state; of the activities rightfully incorporated into "artistic practice" and their value—all persist today. Some are embodied in clashing generations of artists; others live on in our historical imaginaries. The visual arts have always encompassed a wide range of socially and economically valued activities. But it is only in the past few decades that artistic practice underwent the occupational turn that this chapter outlines and came to be seen as ideally a "job" by a majority of participants in the field. Today, a rationalized vision of the proper role and attitude of the artist dominates, despite the contours of a field that retains compelling elements of a very different vision of art work, including living artists who began their careers in a different era. Art has become work, but the rationalization of artistic practice into an increasingly modern job has not been a seamless transition. Tensions between more traditional forms of practice and the demands of an occupational commitment to the arts are visible everywhere in contemporary art worlds. As the next chapters show, conflicts over the valuation of practice draw on these past identities and are reflected in practitioners' diverse accounts of value and its bases. Conflicts take the form of distinct routes to valuation; they do not pit value against values, but aim to include some bases of value while excluding others, and in doing so, they shape the boundaries of artistic practice.

Making Cents of Art

3

I FIRST MET JOSH ON A HOT DAY, weaving through a lush yard to find him at the door of his small house, gregarious, three buttons of his shirt undone. We sat at a broad dining table together and talked, drinking cool water and sharing chocolate bars. I asked him whether he considered his finances when he made new work, and he answered quickly: "Yeah, totally, I always have, I always have. Even when I was borrowing money from the bank to make work, and factoring how I would pay it back and the math that would be required in order to pay it back." He pointed to a particular example to give me a sense of what that math looked like for him: "This photo is going to cost $25,000 to make. And it will be an edition of five, and each one will sell for $15,000, which means that I will make $7,500 for each. Which means that $7,500 times five is the total income, less the investment of $25,000, equals this."[1]

A few days later, across town, I talked with Sophie, who worked sixty and seventy hours a week at her day job to be able to afford the considerable expense of producing her own artwork. Though she told me early in our interview that making a living through her art work was her main goal, later she acknowledged that she had recently withdrawn from the advances of a gallerist known as a dynamic and effective salesman. She told me how excited she was instead to have entered a relationship with a gallery that, as she put it, wasn't particularly focused on sales: "They asked me if they could represent me. And I was super excited because I really like their program-ming and they're just super cool. They're more focused on having consistent programming than on sales. I love their programming." She continued to explain why she chose the gallery that now represents her, emphasizing both her relationship with the gallerists and the way that they allow her to ex-plore new directions in her work: "They're good to talk to about art, which is really important to me. They're like my friends." While Sophie told me more than once that she hoped to make a living at her art work, her choices and the ways she explained them told a different, more complex story, and showed what was really at stake for her: working with people who are "good to talk to," working toward "participation in a discourse I want to be partici-pating in."

There is an enormous diversity in accounts of worth in the art com-munity—some artists make sense of art in monetary terms, while others acknowledge their art work as a sort of credential; some say they "have to" make art, that they just love it, while still others point to relationships as a way of making sense of art. Surprisingly, these differing accounts don't line up with simple categories like education, gender, or even economic suc-cess in the arts—rather, artists use particular accounts of value in patterned ways to *do* particular things with words. This chapter and the next explore the types of account that are widespread in contemporary American artistic practice. They show how each type allows for one "way of being" an artist but also allows for the development of caricatures that teach artists how *not* to be, a process that I will consider in depth in chapter five.

The occupational turn of the past fifty years complicates the issue of valuation in the arts, promoting a few socially dominant accounts of value and delegitimizing others. What does it mean to the valuation of artistic practice that so many artists see what they do as work, as a job—regardless of their credentials, employers, income, or other markers of an occupation? Among artists, four types of account are widespread; I call them *pecuniary, credentialing, vocational,* and *relational* accounts of value. Both pecuniary and credentialing accounts fit a rationalized understanding of the value of work as well as our historical imagination about income generation in the arts before, say, 1900, but the others are harder to fit to an occupational-ized vision of artistic practice. In this chapter, I will consider pecuniary and credentialing accounts before moving in chapter four to a discussion of the arguments implied by vocational and relational accounts.

· · ·

Recall that I said that I would be focusing on narratives of investment in this book. I use the term *investment* here as an analytical category that encompasses a wide range of accounts. These accounts are narratives of investment because everyone expects returns on their resource commitments, though such returns are diverse, diffuse, and unreliable. Artists do not see themselves as burning money or throwing it to the winds, and the artists I spoke with linked future returns to their accounts of investment. They regularly volunteered information on investments they made in their practices. They told stories of money spent, sacrifices made, and choices driven by their practice, and described the processes of deciding what to commit, when to commit, and how to do so.

The artists I spoke with did not often use the terminology of investment that I use when I refer to their narratives, but we should not mistake them for being naïve toward, distant from, or disdainful of cash and calculation. People say that artists don't talk about money, but they just don't talk about money more than others. It's not socially acceptable to go up to a receptionist and, without a greeting, ask how much they make per hour, but many artists encounter such inappropriate queries all the time. The discomfort they experience was summarized nicely in a recent editorial on corporations trolling exhibitions for talent: "Imagine this were a danceclub. . . . Now imagine someone walking into the club, approaching people one by one, inquisitively demanding: 'How can you be had sex with?' "[2] Among themselves, many artists talk about prices—as well as costs, salaries, wages, insurance, child care, rent, deals, and discounts—regularly. Successful artists I spoke with often discussed their finances with me in great detail and reported doing so with others, seeing such "straight talk" as their responsibility to a younger generation that might still grapple with the mythologies of bohemia.

What kinds of investments, then, do I mean? Many artists I interviewed spoke in detail about monetary investments in their practice; these narratives tended toward straightforward accounts of money spent on materials, space to work, and time to work. Cash here is just another finite resource, neither privileged nor ignored. The artists I spoke with often offered hard numbers; there's little mystery here, though outsiders can be shocked by the very high cost of producing some artworks—a hundred dollars for a small tube of oil paint, two thousand for a potter's wheel, several hundred dollars just to frame a completed work. The costs of artistic practice can be high: artists rent and buy specialized equipment; they pay rent on a studio or refurbish the barn; they outsource production, sometimes working with large teams to produce images, objects, or installations. Artists invest in their practices too by intentionally reducing costs—they take low-paying, dull, or otherwise less-than-ideal jobs that offer discounts on or access to prohibitively expensive technology; they spend more on a bigger apartment to maintain an at-home studio rather than pay two rent bills. And of course, artists' investments in their practices don't stop at studio rentals and tubes of paint; for most, the largest investment is in time to work. To have time to work, artists invest finite resources in their practices—they, like others, spend money to free up their own time, paying for child and elder care and hiring assistants—and they discuss intentional cost cutting undertaken in order to prioritize time for artistic practice over paid work.

Artists I interviewed who lived with a partner, and especially those with children, generally talked of complex systems of investment and resource management. Armando told me, "My wife makes more money than me. But I have the flexibility in this job to make sure that I'm not paying for things like day care. . . . I like cooking a lot too, so we don't eat out so much, and that ultimately saves money, and we eat well." Sophie first brought up her boyfriend when she told me about large sculptures she had brought home: "My studio is too dirty to do the work there, which is why I do it at home. Because they have to be really clean. So I—yeah, they're in my house. And my boyfriend is super understanding about it." She laughed; it's silly to even bring him into it, but you can't not. She came back to him when we talked about finances: "My boyfriend is paying more rent than me." She hesitated, maybe a little embarrassed. "We've been together for ten years; we've always split everything evenly . . . we've been talking a lot about what it means for me to me to try to be an artist. And he has to support . . . he has to . . . we can't live the lifestyle that we lived before. Unless he's willing to pay more for it." While some artists I spoke with depended in part on their partners for financial support, others earned enough to support their families. When Kerry told me about his developing sales career, the story he told was one of family finances: After school, he entered a residency program, and that led to a few sales. Galleries started to approach him, and he told me, "It was just like one thing after another and then my wife and I sat and looked at the numbers one day and we said, let's see if we can do this." She had been an elementary school teacher for years, but they thought they might be able to get by on Kerry's sales alone: "We finally said, OK, well, maybe this could work. Let's try it and see what happens. So we did. We moved to a smaller city where the cost of living was less expensive to see if we could make it work." And it had; at the time of our interview, Kerry's wife had been home and taking care of their children for about three years. Such discussions make clear the extent to which, for artists with partners and families, household and family economies are generally what matter, rather than personal income. While this is not specific to visual artists, it does problematize economists' understanding of artists as sometimes subsisting on "family contributions." Assuming that artists primarily benefit from income-generating spouses minimizes artists' noncash contributions to family reproduction, like child care and meal preparation, and ignores artists' cost-reducing practices that contribute meaningfully to family economies.

In my judgment, almost all the artists I spoke with intentionally earned less money than they potentially could have, and this is a major form of investment in artistic practice. I believe such patterns to be true generally—who do you know that values money above all else, really?—but to be especially pronounced among visual artists. I use the word "intentionally" here to indicate that the artists I discuss are aware of their capacity to make more money if they made different choices and that they have chosen not to prioritize higher incomes but *have favored their artistic practices* instead. While a very few argued that a stable job and high income allowed for more creativity and productivity—two, of the eighty I spoke with—generally the artists I interviewed looked for part-time or flexible jobs, and valued such flexibility more highly than income. They regularly took time off from paid work to finish a project or to travel for an exhibition or residency.[3] A number of the artists I spoke with had left well-paying jobs to pursue their art practice, and were always aware of what it had cost them—on average, by moving to less well-paid jobs or to self-employment, these artists had lost half their income. But investments in artistic practice didn't stop at lost wages. These artists were unlikely to have retirement savings, good health care, or the other "perks" of the sorts of jobs they would have been able to get—had often at one point had—if they had not prioritized their artistic practice. But, like Janet, they say it's worth it. She sold her home when she made the leap from finance to a career in the arts: "I was living on the thirty-ninth floor of a beautiful high-rise condo in downtown San Francisco, with my beautiful new Italian white tile floor and my lovely everything." She smirked at that, her other life, and continued: "Today I enjoy my life, and it's at a very modest level. If you're trying to maintain fancy houses and cars, this wouldn't be possible, but . . . if I don't like my boss, it's my own fault."

Most artists I spoke with combined multiple forms of investment in their artistic practices: financial commitments, cost-reducing measures, and the minimization of outside employment. For many, especially for younger artists, this led to the sort of "bohemia" that we sometimes imagine to be a sort of style choice, a bohemia that I will discuss in chapter five. All artists invest something in their practice, and most require monetary as well as nonmonetary resource commitments in order to practice art. Everyone invests something, but expected returns are diverse, diffuse, unreliable, and can be difficult to acknowledge. In the analysis in the chapters that follow I explore patterns in artists' accounts of expected returns on the investments of money, time, space, energy, and other finite resources that all artists devote to their practices.

In the end, artists tend to look much like others who have been devoted to something other than occupational employment, and they are diverse in much the same ways. A parent leaving the workforce to care for a disabled child, a religious seeker traveling to find enlightenment, a grassroots community organizer—all of these people invest in something other than a job, and all of them make the same kinds of choices that artists do.

In my analysis, I use the common strategy of typification.[4] The ideal types discussed in these chapters are not mutually exclusive or personal traits; artists use first one, then another type of account in patterned ways when they account for the value of artistic practice. Different practices are accounted for in different ways, and individuals move both synchronically and temporally between types of account. Some seemed to contradict themselves, saying at one point that they do things for love, at another point that they do it for money; these apparent contradictions will be investigated in depth in chapter five.

I focus on accounts to uncover artists' own perspectives: to understand artists' stated reasons that they did the things that they did, the returns that mattered, the outcomes they aimed for—or, at least, the ones that mattered the day we spoke. As I will discuss below, there is good reason to take artists at their word, for some analyses at least. Envisioning the purpose of artmaking to be making a living at artmaking and denying artists' statements that don't jibe, for example, is a position that makes sense only to the most single-minded and narrow labor, education, and tax policy analysts. In this study, I privilege the way that artists talk about a particular sale over the observable qualities of the sale itself, while gathering data on both. An artist might use a pecuniary narrative to tell me about the sale of an artwork; another might tell me about a sale that looks similar but which they narrate differently. To understand how valuation works, I look to artists' words, and take them seriously.

.   .   .

Artists often speak in instrumental terms: I made this painting in this way because I knew it would sell; I went to art school there because I thought it would be the most direct route to a teaching position. Two types of instrumental account are common: *pecuniary* accounts are tales of investment and return that are clear, specific, and legible even to the most skeptical outsider. *Credentialing* accounts are oriented to a labor market, rather than the market for objects that dominates pecuniary accounts; they are less certain, but similarly legible to the artist's cousin or accountant. Both narrate the ways that the value of artistic practice can be understood in instrumental, often monetary terms—sales made, careers built—but they are, of course, not the only accounts widespread among artists, and their uses are not always as straightforward as they first appear.

I call the most straightforward instrumental accounts of investments and returns pecuniary accounts. They are, for artists, easy to discuss, easy to calculate, and easy for outsiders to understand; they also translate well to an occupational vision of artistic practice. As noted in chapter one, people say that artists don't talk about money, but I find that they simply don't talk about money more than the rest of us do; artists are often able to relay a precise calculus when asked, and regularly offer descriptions of their mental spreadsheets.

Recall Josh, whose words opened this chapter. Josh's narrative, with its calculative clarity and rational tone, is representative of many artists who use pecuniary accounts, as is his narrative's connection to the sale of an object. Sales and—in particular, sales of paintings—dominate pecuniary accounts, even appearing in accounts from some artists who do not use the medium. Making paintings specifically to earn money, even by those who do not focus on painting in their "own work," is a possibility widely acknowledged among artists. Adam, who today does not paint or even draw, told me, "I started making paintings in college to pay for college." He went on, clarifying how painting for money had worked for him: "It was a private school and I had no financial assistance from my family. And so there were rich kids there, some of whose parents were patrons. The school itself would buy paintings from me. Like the administrative departments, to decorate." Sculpture, another traditional medium, is also frequently discussed in bread-and-butter terms. But pecuniary accounts can be used to narrate other, less object-oriented practices as well.

Gregory told me about his shift away from painting driven primarily by financial insecurity: "I started doing performances because as a performer you get a fee." He had been focused on painting, but "when you're making paintings, you put all the money into the production of it, and then you're hoping that this other person helps to sell it, and then you wait for them to clear the check, and then it comes back to you. Performance was the better way to go." He told me about a performance-based project he had developed, and told me why he was pleased with it: "I started that project and, in fact, it was successful in its goal. I get invited by schools and nonprofits and different kinds of . . . the project works anywhere, really." We might imagine that something as ephemeral as performance would be tough to monetize, but Gregory didn't see it that way: "The performance thing is really what saved me as being . . . continuing to be in conversation with other artists, because I didn't have studio space, I couldn't afford to make artwork otherwise." In fact, performances and other apparently ephemeral artworks like projects and videos have been long objectified and commodified in art worlds, and artists who wish to monetize them have a rich history of convention to draw on. Note Gregory's statement of his performance project's "goal"—to be invited to perform, for a fee. Since beginning that project, Gregory's income had normalized somewhat and he had been able to return to painting, but he continued to see a performance practice as a more reliable source of income.

Discussions of hours and wages in paid employment in relation to time and money for art work were widespread in pecuniary accounts. Synnove, who runs a business with her husband, feels that she has to buy out her time in order to paint, so she looks for grant funding: "When I was wanting to extend myself as a painter I looked to state arts funding. I wanted some of that money. So I was thinking, 'OK, projects, projects, what could I do?' I wanted time to paint." For her, time spent painting was legibly time not spent earning money together with her husband—she did the books, after all. "I run my own business, so I felt like I always had to earn my time to paint, because it is downtime. There's no certainty that you're going to sell your paintings, or that you'll make much money from them." All the same, she wanted to paint, so she found a way: "I wanted to be paid to paint. And I was. I got that time and I treated it like a job and said, 'No, can't be in the pottery studio, got to go paint today.' It was a way to give myself time."

Artists using pecuniary accounts often describe their investments and presumed returns with calculative clarity. For some, the accounting was straightforward: cash in, cash out. Others conceived of a more complex art budget, incorporating more noncash resources. Bodie spoke in terms of a family budget, with lines for both his and his wife's art costs and profits as well as income from his day job. Time was at a premium, so "when I know I'm working towards an opportunity that might have money attached to it or whatever, I will use a fabricator for that." But cash was tight too: "Oftentimes when you decide to buy something for a project, you measure it against, I need a haircut, or I need jeans, you know? Because disposable income is so narrow." He and his wife had to balance the budget carefully, but were willing to take some risks—after all, it wasn't just "disposable" income that was in play: "You also think of it in terms of investment—if my wife makes work for an art fair, there's a pretty good chance it's going to sell, so it's an easy decision to say, I am going to spend x on materials for that."

Pecuniary accounts portray the world as a zero-sum game.[5] In pecuniary narratives, artists characterized their colleagues as competitors—something they never did in other types of account. Jason's story of his art career began back in high school, and it began with competition. "There were only two people that stood toe to toe with me in art. We fought and stole from each other. I'd say that environment of competition between me and those two other guys was what made me what I am." Later, we talked about his time in art school, and he called back to those rivals: "I miss those two guys; they would push me farther every day than any professor. Because they were nipping at my heels, and they wanted my spot, and they wanted to beat me. There's no professor that's going to sit there and compete with you." He paused a moment. "I've had them steal my stuff before, but it's not the same." Antonio, too, portrayed the art world as a battle: when we met he was feeling "horrible"; he was a member of a cooperative but they had just informed him that he was no longer allowed to show a particular series with them. I asked why: "My point of view is that it was too good. I was selling too many. I sold like eight, and the next day they told me, 'You cannot come anymore with this.'" He continued, now with his focus on another artist in the group: "When he saw that I was selling them like crazy he was totally jealous. According to the board, it was him that sent a claim to the board. He took pictures of all my work." He told me that it wasn't just that one artist, though. "I have the feeling that it's not only him. There are a couple of guys who want to be number one."

Pecuniary accounts are legible to just about anyone. They draw on the image of the rational, profit-maximizing individual; if they don't immediately make sense to outsiders, they usually do once relevant facts about the vagaries of art careers are clear. Most often, though, they simply are stories that artists tell that "make economic sense." Derrek told me that economic constraints sometimes made aesthetic decisions fairly simple: "I feel like we all have a couple of meters at the house. Like a food meter, a home meter, and a bill meter. Any one of those runs dry any moment, you're dead. So you spend your whole life just pumping change into these things, and you try to do what you want to do on the side." He is primarily a painter, and I asked whether he had any interest in doing mural work, something that was relatively well paid in his area. He answered flatly, "No." I pressed, knowing that he had done them in the past: "Anything like that?" He sighed. "No. I mean, I just signed up for a gig to do a mural on a stairwell just for the income, but . . ." he trailed off. His complicated answer makes perfect sense—economic sense.

Those who use pecuniary accounts can seem honest and straightforward, so easy to understand that they can hide a good deal of the truth. Analysts too ready to accept such calculations on their face can easily be misled, especially if they accept pecuniary accounts unquestioningly or privilege them over other, apparently incompatible accounts. In chapter six, I delve into both of these issues more deeply, but here I will consider quickly whether accounts that appear to clash with observed actions should be dismissed.

Some of those I spoke with were ready to account for investments with pecuniary accounts, whether or not they appeared to use such calculations. Josh, whose confident voice opened this section, verifiably sells work at the prices he cites, but many artists with little sales experience also offered their "equations," usually making calculations based on some combination of material costs, labor time, and idiosyncratic measures of inherent value. Adonis told me about the calculations he and his collaborator made with as much confidence as Josh: "We set an hourly wage that we would give to ourselves, material costs, we make a budget, we save all of our receipts." I ask how much this hourly wage is, and he answers before I've finished my sentence: "$35 an hour, per person." But later he admits that the calculation he offered has little to do with their prices: "I mean, there is sort of like a standard for figurative sculpture, for sculpture of a certain size, at a specific level of entry into the art world, like things go for this much, so we're shooting to be just above that." His account is still apparently just as calculated and rational as Josh's, with a clear orientation to the bottom line, but when I ask Adonis about his vision of success, he lets out a long, low whistle and then answers: "I mean, selling *one thing* . . . ." Adonis and his collaborator have never sold a sculpture. Knowing this, should we assume his accounts, calculations, and stories have no meaning?

One might imagine that such speculative accounts are untethered justifications, with little relationship to reality—that artists simply offer a story that makes sense when questioned. But this assumption tells us little about why some artists offer pecuniary accounts, while others never do, and it tells us nothing about how artists make sense of investments to themselves. In looking to artists' narratives in their entirety, I allow for the possibility that artists can use pecuniary accounts to make sense of their investments even when such investment have not yet paid off in their own experience.

When the artists I spoke with accounted for investment with pecuniary narratives, they might in fact have been pushed toward market activity and sales in a way that other artists might not; bread-and-butter thinking may drive sales activity, ideas driving practice, rather than the other way around. Those who employ pecuniary frameworks without the experience of profit may in fact be pushed toward the sale of objects in order to legitimate their accounts. But as I will show, there are many more types of account available to artists who aim to make sense of their investments. Artists I spoke with who depended on the sale of objects for a large portion of their income often accounted for investments with bread-and-butter accounts, possibly because they were more accustomed to making constant monetary cost-benefit analyses of their choices than some of their peers. But pecuniary accounts were not limited to those relying on sales for income. In fact, such accounts were occasionally well developed among both artists who never sold artworks and artists who argued persuasively that sales meant little in their practices—and furthermore, as noted above, pecuniary frameworks are utilized by those who hope for but have not yet had sales success. Pecuniary accounts are not bound to instrumental action, or to any actions in particular: they are, instead, one meaning among others, one that does specific things when deployed.

In pecuniary accounts, the time implied between investment and return is relatively short and specific. "Clock time," with its attendant busyness and density,[6] structures accounts. Artists regularly use numerical justifications and make on-the-fly calculations in the process of accounting for investments in pecuniary accounts. Such calculations are widely understood as legible outside the field of art, and fit Weber's image of instrumental rationality.[7] These accounts are oriented to a commodity market, a market that trades in art objects. The logic of this commodity market dominates pecuniary accounts, such that when artists use pecuniary accounts, they often fit ephemeral and nontraditional practices to this logic—they speak of performances as "objects," for example. The ideal artwork in these accounts is defined by its salable quality, and the ideal space of such accounts is the commercial art gallery. Pecuniary accounts are deeply grounded in art worlds, and as such their orientation to the public is only partial.

Artists using pecuniary frameworks readily report a sort of simple accounting; resources go in, and resources come out, usually with a bit of profit. Some include more complex variables such as inherent value, local markets, and gift economics, while retaining the straightforward resources-in, resources-out calculative language of pecuniary accounts. When the analyst digs deeply, they might find that an artist's calculations are not as simple as they seem, though the logic of the pecuniary account persists. Many of the artists I spoke with, though, never offered pecuniary accounts at all, even when the sale of objects, so often narrated using such accounts, figured centrally in their artistic practice. But these straightforward accounts are not the only way to account for investment in artistic practice by pointing toward a calculable potential for income.

. . .

The sale of objects is only one way to draw a predictable income from artistic practice. A number of others—teaching and commercial production, for example—either require independent artistic practice or are enhanced by it. When artists account for investment by pointing to such careers, they tell us that some of the value of their artistic practice is in its credentialing function. When artistic practice works as a sort of credential, artists take on more diverse and less calculable risks, but they have access to an array of diffuse outcomes. In teaching and commercial work, for example, we see artists entering the world of market work and paid employment *as artists*, in ways that make sense both to artists themselves (who have for centuries sold artworks, taught others, and applied their skills outside the art world) and in a world of jobs, where selling one's products, skills, and time by the hour or by the piece is a normal way to calculate worth and value.[8]

Teaching is probably the most common way that artists parlay their skills into paid work. Teaching art to adults more or less requires documentation of an active and independent artistic practice. While some people train for careers in art education, these careers are aimed primarily at younger audiences—a master of art education degree prepares you for elementary school teaching, not mentoring MFA students. To teach adults in settings like colleges, universities, and visiting artist or artist-in-residence programs, artists need documentation of their artistic practice, often of an "independent" practice, one not visibly supported by institutional employers. It is with this documentation that artists communicate not only their interests and approach but also their skills and areas of expertise.

John, a tenured art professor, was straightforward when he told me why he went to graduate school: "Because in order to teach at the college level, one would have to have that MFA." But when he expanded on his decision, it was clear that the main thing he had hoped to gain from his graduate program—and the main credential he took away from it—was a well-developed practice. He ended up choosing a program that would allow him "to find myself as an artist because I hadn't really found my own vision for myself yet. For me personally, it was kind of a bit of a birthing process." He talked a little about what he had done there. "It was not easy, finding and embracing ultimately the kind of work that I feel called to do. What was really good was the seclusion. That prompted some deep searching and investigating and thinking and all that kind of stuff." While John felt he needed a credential to teach (though some art professors do not hold MFAs or other terminal degrees), he knew that the practice and body of work he developed during graduate school would be at least as important to his future success.

Many artists don't even begin looking for teaching work until they are midcareer. Alan, for example, worked with video, film, and performance for years before starting to teach. When we met, he was working as an adjunct professor at three different art schools, and hoped to one day make his way to one full-time job. Though his experience teaching was relevant to his goal, he didn't spend much time worrying about pedagogical theory or collating his teaching evaluations, and his MFA program did not address the skills necessary for teaching. He spent, instead, as much time as possible developing his artistic practice, and knew that it was through such practice that he was most likely to earn a tenure-track job.

Indeed, at the highest levels, artistic practice as a credential outstrips all others. Lower-status art programs might emphasize pedagogical training and teaching experience, whereas very high status MFA programs often boast professors with little pedagogical training and no advanced degrees but with stellar international careers. Josh had no teaching experience before his move into the high-status department he led when we met, and he told me that his lack of teaching experience was key to winning his position: "I never taught before. I was not in the adjunct pool, no one knew me, they only knew the work. The only way to teach is to have a career. So I just focused on having a career and never trying to kind of half teach, like, adjunct." Similarly, Sophie told me that as she was only a few years out of graduate school, she wasn't ready to look for teaching work: "I would like to teach. . . . I feel like maybe in five years I could find a teaching job but right now . . . they're like, 'What's your exhibition history?'"

It is clear that for teaching, especially at the university level, artistic practice functions as a crucial credential. The value of artistic practice can be in part understood with an eye to its credentialing and accreditation functions, and some artists account for investments in their artistic practice by pointing toward such credentialing when they tell me they hope to one day teach. But it would be a mistake to believe that just because artistic practice has credentialing functions that artists make art in order to be able to teach. Most artists would reverse the order of influence, and say that they hope to teach to enable a long artistic career. Some, like tenure-track art professor Domingo, do this by contrasting the labor market to the market for objects: "If I started to make art for a gallery then I would say, well, what do they want? And then I start to think about what they want and I would start to make work about that, rather than just going to my studio and making art." He worked in a combination of media and often with site-specific projects; of his work, he said, "I know this is never going to sell. And that's one of the reasons I want to teach; I know I can; now I know I can do it well, and I can make money that way to support my . . . my habit." To understand the significant investments that most of the artists I spoke with devote to their artistic practice, acknowledging the credentialing functions of such a practice helps us to see the diverse and often significantly delayed returns of such resource commitments.

Artists account for investment by pointing to the credentialing functions of artistic practice both for teaching work and for what I'll call here *commercial work*. When artists use that term, they most often refer to moneymaking jobs using artistic foundation skills like commercial illustration. Here, I expand this term to encompass *any* nonteaching employment that uses skills built in artistic practice, even when the skills could be gained in other ways, or when the work in question is far removed from the worlds of art.

Artistic practice is in itself the crucial credential for what artists themselves refer to as commercial work—commercial photography, illustration, design, production ceramics. Although an artist can work in these fields without a fine art background (one can attend specialized degree programs or apprentice to become a commercial photographer, for example) the majority of the artists I spoke with had developed the skills necessary for commercial work through their practice and had done such work at least occasionally. Some had done it for years, especially if they had fallen into a well-paid niche. Sean found work doing product photography after graduate school thanks to his artistic experience with large format photography: "they couldn't find anyone else in town that knew how to work a computer and a view camera at the same time." Very few artists rejected small freelance jobs working for other artists or for friends. As Elaine told me, "I *do* do a little bit of work as a photographer, and it happens to be mostly documenting other artists, other performance work. I don't have any interest in being a wedding photographer or anything like that."

Many artists I spoke with, and a majority of those holding MFA degrees, had worked as assistants to other artists, and for this work, artistic practice is clearly the most significant credential. Though artists often outsource work to non-artists and occasionally hire non-artists as assistants, most of those working as part-time or full-time assistants to individual artists are artists in their own right. Adonis had worked as an assistant to another artist for some time. His background was in sculpture, while his employer's was in painting, and it was his artistic practice that got him the job. At the time of our interview, he worked thirty-two hours a week: "There is a lot of research and development. . . . I engineer all of the things that get made there, so all of the troubleshooting, problem solving, learning how to work with plastics and foams and things like that, that's all my job."

Even when artists' assistants work primarily as administrators, answering e-mails and ordering supplies, these positions are still "close to the action," part of the art world. But artistic skills—photography, drawing, three-dimensional design—are not the only ones widespread among artists that can be applied to commercial work. Artists often find their way to commercial work that requires skills for which they have neither formal education nor employment experience. For these jobs, they show through documentation of their artistic practice that they have the relevant skills. These jobs are often an important piece of some artists' household economies, though the credentialing function of artists' practices is often overlooked in discussions of the relationship between artmaking and employment in what can sometimes seem like unrelated day jobs. Though such work is often overlooked both by analysts and by artists themselves in discussions of the types of commercial work available to artists, artists regularly use skills developed for their artistic practice to find what might be considered esoteric commercial work less obviously related to artistic practice. A number of artists I spoke with talked about their digital skill set as the key to making a living, thanks to the relatively high level of technological skill now needed for some forms of artmaking, such as film, video, and photography. Synnove worked part-time as a librarian, a job she got thanks to skills she developed working with photography. She pulled out an invitation card for an exhibition opening she had finished recently and told me about the design process, then told me how such work had led to her day job in a library: "This has driven me to improve my computer skills, so I'm more employable. That's one reason I was able to get a technical job, which I shouldn't have. I'm obviously not qualified as a librarian."

Other forms of expertise and craft skills also allowed artists to find esoteric commercial employment. Carlton developed niche skills through his art practice, originally film- and video-based, and worked first as a studio technician: "working at an art school in their media area, like purchasing equipment, renting equipment to people, fixing equipment, all that stuff. So that was the thing that I did to get by. And then I would do other odd jobs that were all tech related." A few years later, he went back to art school for an MFA degree and then did some assisting work before dusting off his film skills to land in a strange but well-remunerated niche: "My job was doing 16mm loopers for museums. That was something that I just found out that nobody knew how to do really, or not that many people could do it. So that was a really good supplement." Peter, mainly a sculptor, told me:

"I worked in the newspaper industry for two years as a prepress technician, which, actually, my art degree helped facilitate. That's a good job, a real job." More recently, he had found work in a small engineering firm: "I do a lot of 3D drawings on the computer, so that was kind of how I was able to work. The thing he liked about me is just my inventiveness. He just liked me because I had pretty much done everything." Peter worked in engineering until his job as an adjunct professor was steady and well-paid enough to leave.

Credentialing accounts often revolve around teaching or commercial work, but a third theme was widespread in these accounts as well—that of the artist's temperament. Not everyone points to one-to-one relationships between skills built in artistic practice and market-relevant "hard" skills. Some point, more simply, to something like the artist's temperament as having value. It's not just a jumble of skills, they say, but who you are—the kind of agency you learn you have, the sort of hustle you can bring to almost anything, even a kind of persona that in itself can bring value to almost anything the artist touches. Artists regularly talked about their temperament when they told me how they had found paid work despite a lack of credentials: when Josh told me about an early promotion, saying, "They kind of looked at me and I was, like, *I can do this*"; when Synnove laughed and told me she was "obviously not qualified" for her job as a librarian; when Bodie told me, "I think I can fake it, you know?"

An artistic temperament, it seems, is something like a liberal arts education—it just made you better at *everything*, and most educated people knew that, or so the story went. Artists talked especially about agency, hustle, and personality when they talked about the value of an artistic temperament: about the ways that such a temperament added market value to the artist *as an individual* rather than as a bundle of skills, awards, or other separable objects.[9]

Doug, like others who pointed to their temperaments, thought of himself as a sort of jack-of-all-trades: "If something needs to be fabricated I kind of know how to do that. If something needs to be rewired I kind of know how to do that. A lot of people tend to be very specialized, and I'm a real hacker, craftsperson, handyman, you know. It helps me in a lot of ways." He told me the reasons for his success came down to his mentality: "It's not how well I can do some coding. That's not the way I look at the world. I just kind of look at all the different possibilities, which means that I'm never really good at anything." He laughed. "I guess the school that I got my undergraduate with would call me a gifted generalist." Janet told me she had fallen into everything she had ever done—before becoming a professional artist in her forties, she had a career in finance, had been a vice president at one of the world's largest banks. When she described that career, just as when she talked about her move into the arts, she shrugged: "I've been totally unqualified to do anything I've ever done, and I just don't let that bother me."

Talk of the artist's temperament regards the artist's personality, their very self, as a sort of transferable skill or credential, as a brand with value. It was Gregory's use of an odd phrase—the "commodity fetishism of my personality"—that helped me to see what he and some others were talking about. Looking back through Gregory's interview, that notion was everywhere, as here, when he spoke of his day job: "When I work there, the company then gains a very sophisticated perception as being connected to a very thoughtful kind of art slant." He used the value of his persona to bargain with—and threaten—his employers: "In these negotiations with my job, I always just say, like, 'oh, I just want to get paid to be The Gregory, you know. If I don't get to do it here I'll do it somewhere else.'" He went on, saying that what mattered was "something kind of intangible," that despite working "*very* seriously with materials and materiality and stuff like that, it's like . . . What I do is, I portray this kind of, I don't consider it utopic; I think empathetic is a more accurate term for what it is that I'm involved in. I portray a certain kind of empathetic lifestyle." He tried to articulate its value: "It's close to you, and it touches on sensuality, and memory, and community, and all of these different things, and it's like, I just basically portray that in different ways. That's the real thing, the actual . . . that's what I bring to whatever it is."

Like Gregory, Derrek joined together narratives about agency, hustle, and personality when he told me what he brought to the table as an artist. He started out by telling me about what differentiates artists from other people: "To be a professional artist, you don't find jobs. You have to have the talent to be able to create jobs around you to fit you. That's a skill that not everyone has, but I think artists have it better. You have to be a really a good delegator and a network builder." He switched suddenly to a story about going into the military halfway through art school: "When I was in the Army I went overseas to the desert. While I was there, alcohol was illegal. It's like prohibition. If you get caught with it, dire consequences. I saw people work out in the desert for six months for no pay for having alcohol. You could . . . it was *bad*." What he said next showed me how the agency, sense of hustle, and personality of the artist can be used to exploit even the most structured institutions: "I was in a Special Forces unit and our neighbors were the German Special Forces, who had a *warehouse* of alcohol. I was one of the four Americans allowed on their base, because I exchanged supplies with them. So I found myself in a position to start running an illegal beer market, a black market." He smuggled "thousands and thousands of dollars' worth of alcohol to the American base." It wasn't easy: "To do that, you have to find drivers. You have to find people to hand it off, people who want it. You have to be just casual friends with the Germans. You have to learn how to casually make friends with people to get these networks." Being in the Army taught him about working as an artist: "The biggest lesson I learned was how important networking is. You need to network with people, you need to learn how to tactfully just be friends, for mutual benefit, and work together to get things done. I think that the same principle applies with making a living as an artist."

Credentialing accounts share some features with pecuniary accounts: they, too, are structured by clock time, are legible outside the field of art, and are highly grounded in art worlds, with only a minimal orientation to the public. However, credentialing accounts deviate from pecuniary accounts in a number of ways. The time implied between investment and return is long and uncertain, and while calculations abound, numerical justifications are seldom used. These accounts are oriented to a labor market, where skills have value; thus, these accounts straddle the line between instrumental and value-rational logics, between working for income and occupation as identity. The ideal art work in credentialing accounts is defined by its technical superiority, and the ideal space of these accounts is the art academy.

Artists don't make art *in order* to teach web design any more than they make art just to be able to sell art. Exceptions may occasionally prove the rule, but in general, artists' market activities come subsequent to their artistic practice and are undertaken in order to support it. I expected artists to be more comfortable talking about credentialing than about bread-and-butter issues—after all, no one wants others to think that they do anything "just" for the money, and many credentialing accounts allow for some distance from filthy lucre. But I found just the opposite.

Pecuniary accounts were widespread, straightforward, and easy to see and to understand in my conversations with artists. Credentialing accounts were less common, often murky, and often relayed with a bit of a squirm. Looking again and again over transcripts, I began to see that some artists used these two types of account together in ways that, when overlaid on what I was able to observe of their practices and their lives, pointed to an interesting sleight of hand. Artists' apparent emphases on prices and pricing made me question much of the literature's focus on art prices as a window on value in the arts.

. . .

In Armando's studio in a medium-sized city in the Northeast, I was surrounded by his work: large abstract oil paintings, heavily textured, hung to the ceilings. He pushed a button on a boom box and perched on a stool as soft jazz rolled across the room. Armando made a living as an artist, and hadn't had a day job for some time. After a while, I asked about the way that he set prices for his paintings and he told me about his "formula," based on their size and the time they took to produce. As our interview progressed, his formula slowly fell apart. He noted that though they should really have been be included, materials fell out of the calculation long ago: "The supplies are really expensive. You can get small tubes of paint that cost easily $60. The investments to make them, I have to stop thinking about them. Because if you're always thinking about how much each one is costing, it limits you. And you can't be limited by that." I asked how he set the hourly rate he used, and he hemmed and hawed a moment before acknowledging, "I haven't done the time equation in a while. That's a real tough one. That's a real tough question." I asked about the prices of particular works in the studio, and it was clear that if he even motioned toward the calculation of labor and dimensions he said he made, he would have needed to charge much more than he did—even assuming poverty wages, which is a lot to ask of someone with a master's degree, significant education debt, and a family to support. He told me about the last painting he had sold, and it turned out he had sold it on credit: "I try to make it really easy for people; if they want to purchase something, I give them as much time as they want. Like, I sold a painting, and I haven't had any of the money come in yet for it. It was $800, and I just told them that whenever they had it, they could send it to me."

Armando did sell paintings, but not often and not at prices that begin to cover his significant investments. But if we look at more than his paintings and their prices, we see a diverse practice, a sort of portfolio career with a range of paid and unpaid activities. Armando taught art privately to children and adults, and his studio doubled as a classroom. He made a living teaching, and occasional income from the sale of an artwork is a pleasant bonus, even as the production of such artwork was central to his working life. Occasional income from residencies, fellowships, and commissions rounded out the picture. One way to understand Armando's painting practice is by acknowledging his paintings as credentialing his teaching work in two ways: first, as training, since he wouldn't be able to teach if he weren't a skilled painter, and such skills require development and upkeep; second, as a display of his skill, since prospective students and their parents need evidence of his ability in order to enter into a tuition-paying relationship. His artwork demanded significant time, and had led to his leaving high-paying work for a more precarious existence. But he and his family got by, and had just bought a house. We may wish to understand Armando as a calculating actor and to take an instrumentally rational view of his actions. The analyst looking only to prices may not be able to make sense of Armando as a calculating artist, while the analyst willing to look beyond price will see an artist's career where the $60 tubes of paint, the monthly rent on the studio, and the foregone wages he could earn elsewhere all return to economic sense. But one problem remains: how should we understand the false calculations that he offered when I asked about his prices, and his readiness to offer them?

While many artists I spoke with readily offered coherent pecuniary narratives, they were often less forthcoming in their uses of credentialing frameworks—recall Armando's immediate offer of his "formula" for pricing. Since Armando worked independently as a teacher, running his own school, I thought he might be similarly forthcoming about his hourly wage for teaching, but found that he had trouble explaining how he came to the number. He told me that figuring out what to charge for his teaching was "always difficult." He said, "I set my prices competitive to the other art schools in the area. Except because I'm individually teaching people, and it's not like a group class effort . . . but I don't want art to be something that is only the bastion of people that are able to afford it. . . . I don't want this to be just like a privileged arena." His hourly wage for teaching was quite low in my estimation, based on my knowledge of the local context and his skill level both as a painter and a teacher. Another artist I interviewed with her own teaching studio, Azadeh, was ready to talk about her paintings and the process of showing and selling them, but vague about how she calculated her hourly teaching wage when pressed: "I kind of charge by the hour. . . . Somebody, for instance, they want to talk to me because they're a photographer and they're really stuck and they want to talk to me about what their work means and what materials to use to take it to the next level, and I know they can pay. . . . So I'm probably going charge them a lot of money for that per hour. More than a therapist." Both of these artists maintained two income streams, each requiring significant ongoing investment. Both made and sold paintings with some success, and both taught art individually to children and adults. Both made their living primarily through teaching. And in a pattern visible among artists I interviewed who used credentialing frameworks to account for investments in their artistic practice, they often initially offered pecuniary narratives about the sale of paintings that they readily dismissed on further inquiry.

I found that while artists who leaned heavily on pecuniary logics were easy to identify, narratives that relied on credentialing frameworks often required more interpretive work. Specifically, artists often offered early pecuniary accounts and answers to my questions that they later contradicted—often pointedly, directly, and with a laugh. Taken as a whole, their narratives involved complex accounts of investment that used a credentialing framework, even as they very quotably posed as using pecuniary logics. Those straightforward pecuniary accounts, on interrogation, sometimes appeared to work primarily to distract the listener's attention.

Even though in the popular imagination artists treat bread-and-butter talk as taboo, many artists understand pecuniary frameworks as legitimate, provided that they meet some number of often idiosyncratic criteria. Artists' abilities to quickly evince pecuniary calculations, even when they are unwarranted, point to the ways that such subculturally legitimate calculations can function as a cover for other forms of rationality.

Credentialing accounts are characterized by a high level of ambivalence. There is a perception among both artists and outsiders that dual careers are risky and that commercial work can pollute fine art work. One artist I interviewed uses a pseudonym for his commercial work and told me that whereas others were dragged down by their commercial reputations, he was "*luckily* smart enough, because I surely wasn't smart in other departments in my brain, to know to do nondisclosure agreements." Many artists I spoke with referred disparagingly to other artists that they saw as unduly focused on teaching and commercial careers. Doug referred to his brother, an art professor, as a teacher who exhibits work to "keep up his credentials." Barb told me she cried when she realized her daughter would be an artist, because she envisioned her falling into teaching and doing "shit work"; she referred to a stereotype of the teaching artist who, to keep their job, needs to do, as she put it, "the same old stuff over and over again, and who, at the end of their career, stand up for their final little whatever and then they're out." Mark echoed her when he told me why he didn't want to be an academic, though he loved teaching: "A lot of professors, they get a job, they get tenure, and then they don't make enough work to worry about."

These sorts of concerns, raised regularly in my conversations with artists, serve to enforce subcultural norms about the appropriateness of credentialing frameworks. While direct discussions of credentialing processes were uncommon, when I asked less directly about the ways that artists' practices influenced other parts of their lives, I found artists to be very aware of the impact of their practice on other activities, especially their ability to teach and to do commercial work. Still, many offered straightforward pecuniary accounts that made little sense before acknowledging the credentialing functions of their artistic practice and artworks.

Pecuniary accounts can offer individual artists a means of signaling occupational commitment, both within and outside the art community, without confessing to subculturally illegitimate practices. As I've noted, people think that artists don't talk prices, when they really just don't talk prices all the time, or with all audiences. But the artists I interviewed truly didn't talk about the credentialing and accreditation functions of their art practices very often, and I find such talk to be a much bigger taboo within the community. For artists who hope for, expect, or need a financial return from the investments made in their practices, talking prices is not as taboo as it might seem; talking credentials, on the other hand, is genuinely blasphemous. Peek beneath the surface, and it's often easy to see how thin and flimsy the scaffolding of straightforward bread-and-butter accounts can be. Pecuniary accounts can function as the beard for credentialing logics, hiding them in plain sight behind a polite nod to community mores. They can serve to make messy, diffusely valuable credentialing activity legible, but they are not particularly convincing for the investigator willing to peek behind the façade.[10] Most artists are aware that a greatly diverse group of artists sell objects; pecuniary accounting per se is almost never grounds for dismissal. Investments in artistic practice for the purpose of acquiring or maintaining a credential, however, are real sacrilege.

Artists, like others, understand the economic value of their work in diverse ways. They talk about money like everyone else, though some surprising subjects really are taboo: the line on the résumé, the teaching artist's exhibition. But how do artists balance economic value with other values? What happened to that old, honorable vision of art for art's sake?

Making Sense of Art

4

ABBIE'S STUDIO IS IN A SMALL CAPITAL CITY, one not well known for its art scene, in a very large studio complex. Her space was big, clean, well-organized; the walls were hung with her work, mainly layered images with natural motifs, collage-like, somewhat muted. A few sculptures stood in the corners. Everything was very well made and somehow soothing. We sat at a very large worktable covered with a dropcloth, a few intricately folded bits of paper scattered around the legs of my chair. Abbie was friendly, and forward, and matter-of-fact. Late in our interview, in a soliloquy that could serve as a model either of the importance of knowing the color of your parachute or of the perils of do-what-you-love ideology, Abbie talked about how closely her work was tied to her sense of self as she told me about her family: "My brother in law is a computer geek, and math-based, and I used to have discussions with him that . . ." She paused, and sucked in a long, loud breath. "The discussion centers around, are you doing what you are doing because you want to, or because you have to? Because there is a certain amount of being an artist that feels like 'have to' rather than 'want to,' right? If you were doing this just because you wanted to, it would be a hobby, right? That's the definition of a hobby, right? It's a pastime that you want to do." Her gaze was direct. "But there is a certain amount of being an artist that is deeper than that. I mean, yes, I do *want* to do it but I *want* to do it because I *have* to do it; it's the way I process information. It's that deep of a part of who I am that I can't really process the things that hap-

pen in my life unless I do it through this process. That's the way it works."
She returned to her brother-in-law: "We would have these discussions about,
was I really *lucky* because I got to spend all this time doing what I want to do,
and I would say, well, yes, but . . ." She laughed. "But there is not that much
choice involved, you know; I mean, I kind of *have* to do it. I tell myself stories
about why I am making certain sacrifices, because in order to have time to
work, you have to make sacrifices, but it's really just a story to tell myself to
make up for the fact that I have to do it anyway, because it is who I am."

Artists don't always talk about the value of the things they do in terms
of dollars and jobs. *Vocational* accounts fit the widely held assumption that
artists "have to" create, that they do it "for love, not money," that artists enjoy
art work and that practice is its own reward. *Relational* accounts hearken
back to long-held moral arguments about the beautiful and the good; they
promote artistic practice for the benefit of society as a whole, and for both
artists and audiences as citizens. Looking to these evaluative accounts along
with pecuniary and credentialing accounts to explore expected returns on
investments lets us see how artists make sense of their commitments to
complex and rich artistic practices.

Evaluative accounts can seem more difficult than pecuniary and credentialing accounts to fit to occupational practice and its valuation, but they
have strong relationships with our historical imaginaries about traditional
practice and traditional values and valuation. This does not imply that they
reflect only old meanings. These types of account may point backward, but
their forms are not historical; their expressions are contemporary, their contours more retro than antique. Vocational accounts reach back while relational accounts reach forward and promote new pathways to valuation, but
both draw on historical imaginaries for their legitimacy. Both kinds of account are highlighted by artists as they engage in conflict over valuation.
Through such accounts, they insist on the importance of diverse orders of
worth and work to renegotiate the value of artistic practice.

. . .

Abbie told me, in so many ways all at once, that she feels called to artistic
practice: she has always done it; she has to do it; it's how she thinks, how
she acts in the world. Many artists find returns in the autonomy, integrity,

and tolerance for specificity that an artistic practice can allow. In vocational accounts, artists acknowledge the hard work and sacrifices of artmaking, but consider the work fundamentally rewarding—and often argue that such rewarding work is in itself repayment enough for the resources committed to their practices. These artists account for investments by pointing to the high value of meaningful work (a value widely acknowledged as central to workers in many occupations[1] and occasionally accounted for by cultural economists[2]). As a group, they tend to find the notion of "working for the weekend" laughable.

Artists using vocational accounts positioned art work in opposition to "regular" employment, even when they held such employment and reported that they enjoyed and were challenged by their day jobs. Many offered horror stories of the indignities of such regular employment. These artists did not generally live outside the world of paid work, but used these stories to show by comparison the value of an artistic practice.[3] Kerry had worked in a wide range of jobs, some for years, before moving to full-time work in the arts. But he emphasized his short-lived career as a barista when I asked about his employment history: "I was at Starbucks for a day before I was like, I can't do this. I just, I can't, I can't do this. And it was still in the middle of the training. They were making us taste coffee. And they were trying to get us to talk about coffee in the proper way and everything." He grinned before continuing: "They asked me to taste a cup of coffee and I tasted it and I was like, 'Oh my God, this tastes like dirt.' And the lady's like, 'You . . . no. Don't tell the customers their coffee tastes like dirt.' I'm like, 'No, it tastes like dirt; I'm sorry, it tastes like dirt.' She says, 'No, no, no. You say it's earthy, it tastes earthy.'" He laughed. "Like, OK, fine, you call it that if you want to. But I'm going to call it dirt." He quit that same day: "After that, I left at lunch, and I was like, I'm not going to do this. This is ridiculous."

The stories artists told about these ideal-terrible day jobs had the feel of practiced arrangements; I almost always got the sense that these horror stories had been told before; they didn't have the pauses, disfluencies, and trackbacks common to the rest of the interviews. I came to view such stories as little totems, used regularly by interviewees that displayed them to show by counterpoint the features of artistic practice and the value of meaningful work. While we might imagine artists moving away from market relations entirely or agitating for the downfall of capitalism, I didn't speak with anyone who hadn't already made some sort of peace with market economies, and no one argued that artistic practice was the only path to meaningful work. When interviewees rejected something as "corporate" or "capitalist," they generally referred more specifically to a culture of economism and inappropriate striving. Vocational narratives did not place art outside of market relations, instead, they pointed to a common feature of artistic practice—meaningful work—that the artists saw as less plausible in occupations more closely tied to the demands of markets. Nearly all of the artists I spoke with either held paid employment or made a living through their art work; artists, like others, make life work under capitalism. But in talking about the returns on investments in their artistic practice, even those whose monetary returns were significant often pointed first to the meaning they find in that practice and what they perceived as its scarcity in regular employment.

Artists using vocational accounts valued the possibility of autonomous work in artistic practice, and contrasted such rewarding labor with alienated employment in language that could have come from Marx—and like Marx, the artists I spoke with often seemed to see work as a fundamental human activity, not as a tiring necessity to be offset by leisure and rest. Rosemary told me, "I love working. I've had jobs where the work that I was doing was not core to my creative or intellectual process and where the authority was so far removed outside of me that it was alienating. I've been alienated at work. And to have work that's not alienating is a real privilege." Doug told me that he didn't plan to retire: "I'd just like to continue experimenting with life the way I am now. . . . I'll have all my retirement fun during my entire life, rather than waiting until the very end." Rudy told me, echoing many others, that since he enjoyed painting it wasn't real work: "It works for me because I really love doing it. It's not work for me." He said he "didn't make it into a job," but that doesn't mean he avoids commerce: he shows his work in galleries, works hard at his painting, and sells paintings and work in other media. As Rudy used the term, a "job," like "regular work," simply stood in for all that he didn't like about some of his past employment, and as counterpoint to what he saw as valuable in artistic practice. Those who used vocational accounts to tell me about the value of artistic practice generally didn't shy away from labor, but they were often unsatisfied by work that they saw as insufficiently meaningful. Artistic practice was seen by these artists as inherently rewarding. Armando neatly summarized a common sentiment when he told me, "When I say time for myself, I mean time for my work."

Some artists argued that they simply *were* artists and always had been— often recalling a story from childhood to make this point. Jason told me, "Since I was three years old, I've been drawing. I was in kindergarten and it was time to bring out all the coloring books, and I grabbed mine and threw it on the floor and went over to the typing machine and pulled out a sheet of paper and started coloring on that." He grinned. "The teacher comes over and takes my typing paper away and puts the coloring book in front of me, and I was like, 'I don't want to color. Coloring's not for me.' My mom says I've always been an art snob." So many artists reach back to childhood when they talk about their practice that some joked about it a bit. Henry grinned and asked if I wanted his "origin myth," and then said he had two: one from early childhood and one from his college days. He said both were equally true. Later he referred, a little embarrassed perhaps, to his story of preschool artmaking as "the wee little origin myth." Having always done art—having been a baby painter—was a story widespread among artists who reported having something like a "calling" for artwork. Another dimension was a sense that they "had to" make art—as when Josh told me he had realized that he had to find a way to make art his profession "at *any cost*"—as if the activity of artmaking itself had qualities that gave them something they could find nowhere else. Peter started out talking about his work ethic but ended up telling me about something like a compulsion: "To be a serious artist means that you don't have any spare time. I don't know, it's kind of like, I *have* to be making stuff. It's not like . . . I'm not thinking about, oh, I have a show coming up. I'm making this project. If I show it, that's great."

A sense of a calling is not the only dimension of the vocational narrative; there are others. Some artists even specifically rejected the notion of a calling, as Amy did: "I've *never* been the person who is like, I would die without this, because I wouldn't. I could never make another piece of art, I'd be OK. I'd do something else. I wouldn't die. I'm not that kind of person." Amy rejected the idea that she *needed* to make art, while adopting other vocational language. At another point in our interview, she told me about her most recent project: "I had ideas that were three-dimensional, and I pursued them, even though they were *completely* out of my comfort zone in terms of execution. Like, I had no idea how to really make these things." She had to hire assistants, and then sent the work out to be fabricated: "I had to really figure out how to do it, and I did the wax dipping all by myself. So I created the wax molds all by myself, and then I handed it off to a bronze person." All because she believed in the work: "*I* thought they were going to be good pieces." In the end, they sold well, and she was glad they did: "I'm just proud that I went with this gut . . . I was like, this is a good idea, these are beautiful and funny and smart, and I believe in them and I'm going to invest money that I don't have and take that risk." Her position at the time of our interview—in midcareer, with gallery representation for the first time— made her even more proud of the gamble: "I feel proud that I can take those kinds of risks; especially, I think you hit a certain age and then people expect something from you. If you step outside of that expectation, it can go either way, but very rarely is it lukewarm. Like it's either, 'Oh, she just blew it, who does she think she is,' or, 'Wow, good for you, reinvention.'" Over the years, she had created a structure that allowed her to take these kinds of risks: "I have a gallerist who is open to that. I have friends who—their gallery wouldn't ever let them do something like that. It's like, 'no, you make pictures that cost $50,000, keep making them. [She laughed.] You can't make a *thing*. An object.' So I feel proud of that." Amy did something challenging well, perhaps against her better judgment, and the fact that it worked out in her economic favor simply supported her longstanding practice of going with her gut, maybe made it an easier story to tell, one that others would find easier to understand. Doing something impossible well, especially when others are skeptical, was visible as a source of pride, enjoyment, and value in the accounts of all who offered vocational accounts.

Artists using vocational narratives often told me that they had found themselves engaged in issues that they experienced as too specific, too esoteric for the marketplace. Some argued that only artistic practice allowed for the sort of deep, long-term, open-ended commitment they felt was necessary. They used terms like "exploration" and "research" to describe their practices, and found such work intrinsically rewarding. Sophie told me that following her interior compass was the rewarding part of her practice; she said her work was "super interior, which I think is a result of the specific things I'm interested in," and that she would "rather be making work that is interesting to me, than making work that I think will sell." She elaborated: "I think that probably a lot of people find my work inaccessible. My work isn't for everybody. I know that. It's *really* not for everybody. It's not even for everyone who's into art, who is into contemporary art, that's dealing with the issues I'm dealing with." She makes work to solve problems she's interested in: "Instead of making work that I think is more accessible, I would rather make work that is really delving into the issues that I want to work with. I like to think about the material resistance to my ideas and what it means to be making what I'm making, more than, like, 'How will this be received?'"

Artists using vocational accounts often value following their own muse so strongly that they claim the audience for their work is nearly irrelevant to their practice. Iris told me her artmaking was not oriented to viewers: "If I'm happy with a piece, I don't care who sees it; I don't care what they think about it. I'm just *not attached* to other people's opinions." Adam had, over the years, intentionally narrowed his potential audience in order to preserve and promote the specific ideas he wanted to work with: "As an artist, you're always trying to . . . you *should* be, I think, trying to pay attention to what you *need* to continue. Like what do you think of as successful? Do you need six people to care about what you do? Do you need books to be written about what you do? What do you need? Do you need your mom to come to your opening?" He told me that when he had left his galleries, ten years before we met, he realized he "only needed about four or five people to care about what I was working on. They needed to be committed to the same type of work I was involved in, but I didn't need that many, and I didn't need the galleries. I didn't need the magazines. I needed just enough to keep the dialogue going." And he saw a precedent for his way of working: "I'd always been impressed with these ideas, like Leibnitz and people, who were working on mathematical problems and they would write it down in a certain number of manuscript copies and circulate it to other people who cared about the same stuff, and this idea that that was enough to keep it going."

Themes of a sense of a calling and the ability to follow esoteric muses recurred in vocational narratives. A third theme recurred, and this was by far the most widespread; it can be seen, above, in Amy's pleasure at risks taken.

All of those who used vocational accounts pointed to their ability to take joy in the process of creation—no matter the outcome—and pleasure in meeting self-determined challenges as key to understanding the value of artistic practice. Jay told me, "I always say my job is to be dissatisfied." He is a glassblower, and as we spoke he and an assistant maneuvered huge, heavy lumps of burning glass in and out of furnaces, the molten knurls always looking as if they were about to fall off his tools into disaster. I asked what a good day looked like, and he glared playfully at his assistant: "It's a good day when there's nothing on the floor. Three out of five days this week we've had a big piece go on the floor." He laughed, and then went back to speaking seriously: "That's all right, I like crashing noises. You have to love crashing noises. You know you're pushing the edge." His assistant muttered, "Wrong side of the edge." Jay chuckled at him, and disagreed: "It's like taking the wheelbarrow out to the edge: you dump a little more sand and the path gets longer."

After Barb told me that she finally, in late career, had the confidence to do what she wanted, she told me about several of her new projects. Though she was at an age and career stage where she probably would have been able to coast on her skills and accomplishments, each new project she told me about involved learning new things—a challenge that she specifically pointed to as valuable: "I took on some of those monumental exhibitions. Huge exhibitions. There's a lot of engineering with that work, a lot of iron-work underneath, a lot of . . . major crating, a lot of huge moving skills. That can be exhausting, but really exciting. Really exciting knowing how to do all that stuff. And pull that off." She told me about how privileged she felt, but also that constantly challenging herself could be difficult: "I get exhausted, and I usually . . . I have lupus underneath everything, and so I always end up in the hospital." She laughed, and continued: "But it's hard not to just rise to the occasion completely when you've got an exhibition." She had recently started on a new project, a public commission, "nothing like anything I've ever done. And my assistant thought I was crazy when I took it on." But she wanted the challenge: "I wanted the experience, and I just sort of went and did it, because I really wanted to learn how to do it. It was the first time I had ever done it, I didn't know how it was going to work. And I did it for a kick." Barb pays high costs to be able to work hard, to learn new things, to rise to the challenges she sets out for herself. She has significant health problems and knows that if she exhausts herself she will end up ill; she takes on projects today that don't begin to pay for her time or materials. But learning new skills and taking on new challenges is important enough to her to make it all worth it. To Barb, and to the other artists who used vocational accounts in their conversations with me, the process of artmaking—a difficult process, with self-imposed barriers at every step—is its own reward.

A number of artists with experience in other professional arenas compared the sorts of challenges artists were willing to take on with the relative risk aversion of others. Peter, who had originally planned to become an academic physicist, contrasted his practice directly to the kind of life he might have had. He started by talking about how hard it is to sell anyone on a project before it's completed: "It's always like whatever makes sense to me doesn't make sense to a lot of people." He had recently met with a physicist and told her, "'Oh, I wish I had gone the physics route, and then now I'd be so much better at my projects.' She said, 'Yeah, but you wouldn't make them, because you would know they wouldn't work. The only reason they work is because you actually do them, right? If you knew that they wouldn't work ahead of time, you would never do anything.'" Peter wasn't the only one who told me a story like this.

Domingo had a good deal of experience working with engineers and scientists. He told me that artmaking for him was all about challenging himself: "If I were just doing the same thing over and over again, I get tired, and bored. That's probably why I want to be an artist, because I can . . . not necessarily do what I *want*, but do things that I'm really interested in." Much of his work involves modifying existing consumer electronics, usually well beyond recognition. During a residency at one institution famous for the creativity of its research and public programming, he told me that even the research staff were "so structured and so confined" that when he asked the senior scientists there for help with his project, they dismissed him out of hand. "They said, that's never gonna work. And I was like, OK, thanks for your help." He laughed, and then went on: "But like three months later, I kind of got it to work, and it was working, and I said, hey, come see this, and they were like, whoa." That piece got the attention of a large corporation, and he went in for a meeting with them. They offered him access to new technology still in development that was unavailable to the public. But he immediately realized that they were just as risk-averse as the scientists he had worked with before, and said he had "the worst experience." He told the company's engineers what he wanted to do, and they were unimpressed. "The engineers are saying, that's never going to work. And I said, great! Let me try it! But they just . . . I don't see that going anywhere." Domingo had found that those outside the art community didn't have the same commitment to tackling difficult challenges as his friends in the arts did. He summed up the difference between himself and the scientists he'd worked with succinctly: "I do things that most likely other people wouldn't do."

I asked Josh to tell me about something recent that he had done that he was particularly pleased with, and he told me about going to a writers' colony to create a prospectus for a large project he was starting, one that required a written plan. He said it was hard because he wasn't a good writer, and scary too. "And painful because when you are doing something you don't know how to do, it's like playing Jenga with your fingers missing." But he was pleased; it was "something I had not done before. So that's . . . I think the older you get the less often you do things that you haven't done before." There was "no blueprint." The exact wording of the question I'd asked was, "Can you tell me about something that you did recently that you're particularly happy with?" Josh, like so many others I spoke with, told me more about a process than a product—and described a "painful" process akin to competing with a crucial handicap.

The artists who used vocational accounts when they told me about their artistic practice often prioritized the challenges they valued, even at great cost and risk to themselves and their artistic practice. Barb, as discussed above, lost money; sometimes she ended up in the hospital. But it worked out. Doing something seemingly impossible well—especially when others were skeptical—was visible as a source of pride, enjoyment, and value in the narratives of all who offered vocational accounts. Just as physicians might point to meaningfulness as the central quality of their occupation while also drawing a high salary, artists who valued meaningful work often look for or create ways to engage in meaningful work that is also rewarded by the market. But for those whose artistic practice does not engage as successfully with the worlds of goods and services, placing a high value on meaningful work (and finding it only in nonmarket artistic practice) can mean nonmarket work makes perfect sense, even when its precedence over paid work causes problems. Peter made us both laugh when he told me: "I'm one of those people that I'm just always working. Which is hard financially." This sentiment, perhaps on its face a bit confusing, is recognizable to most artists, as well as to most others who try to balance significant commitments outside paid employment with market demands on their time, energy, and other resources.

Vocational accounts differ strongly from either pecuniary or credentialing accounts. Time is irrelevant to narratives of investment and return; it is suspended, transcendent, and has much more in common with the task-oriented time described by E. P. Thompson, including its lack of division between "work" and "life," than it has with modern, regulated clock time.[4] Numerical and calculative justifications do not appear in these accounts. Even though the practices discussed in vocational accounts are relevant to the labor market, these accounts are not oriented to the labor market, and in part thanks to this, they are often illegible to those outside the field as legitimate explanations of investments. These accounts can be categorized as value-rational narratives, with institutional foundations (however distant) in religion,[5] and the ideal space of such accounts is the home studio—domestic, but set apart from everyday life. There is no ideal artwork in vocational accounts. In fact, the outcome of artistic practice is often minimized as irrelevant. Vocational accounts of investment and return have no public orientation, nor do they point directly to any art worlds.

. . .

In 2012, I visited Alan at his home on the West Coast. His apartment was up a narrow staircase, and inside it was clean, white, spare, and very bright. We went back to a kitchen to sit, and Alan poured me some coffee he had made in a press. We talked for a good while before I turned on my recorder, finding mutual acquaintances. I asked him what it was like for him when he moved to the area, and he grimaced. "I felt like it took a while to get accepted into a circle. And a couple of people were way more welcoming. I started more in-depth friendships with them. And making stuff and talking with them more." The relationships he built took time: "By being generous with others, and creating opportunities for other people that I wanted to work with, that I thought they were making fun stuff, or I thought they were being generous in other ways with other people, those were the people I wanted to work with." He started a small presenting institution and supported other artists' work: "Doing that for a year solid and doing it every other month for two to three more years, I think I became way more present within the community."

When Alan told me about projects he had done and people he had met, he always focused on the close relationships he formed—not the networking, or the events he had been a part of, the art he had made or his sales or fees, but the relationships. He told me someone saw his videos, and liked them; the result: "that started some friendships and stuff." He did a project with artists in another city, and situated it art historically in intimacy: "It's kind of like these early versions of performance artists of the '70s, going down there and coming up here and having exchanges. There's a real warmness in the people." I asked about a long-term project he was engaged with that involved other artists. He told me it was relationships that counted: "It's trying to work with somebody I want to spend more time with, or talk with, and stuff, instead of it being just like, 'I need to do a show.' It's like, no—I don't need to do a show." We talked about his life in and out of art institutions, and he told me why he kept one foot in the door, why he continued to work with traditional institutions though so much of his work—and so much of where he finds meaning—happens, and stays, outside of them. "Do you want to make a living from your work, or do you want to make a contribution? I keep . . . I think just that word, 'contribution,' is something that keeps coming back to me." He worked as an adjunct professor, and said that this issue was central to him both as an artist and as a teacher: "I think this past year was one of the first times I saw a few students that I think will continue to do some creative endeavor more long term. That are doing substantial things. And that makes me feel like I'm more connected to this generational history that's happening. Which is exciting to me and gives me meaning in a lot of ways." The idea of generational time influenced his relationships with other artists as well. "Reaching out cross-generationally to artists of the area or outside this area and having more extended conversations with them and befriending them and having more in-depth conversations with them, it's not just being written about in a book." He searched for a word, and then continued: " 'Camaraderie' is maybe a better word for what I'm kind of after.

I don't want to say a legacy, but something where there's that extended cama-raderie that's cross-generational. That the people that you admire or really appreciate in terms of what they've done with their work, you're a part of that conversation and you're part of that kind of extension and they under-stand what you're up to more than other people will. Those things give me a lot of happiness."

After the taped interview we talked some more, about all kinds of things. Eventually I had to leave, and he walked me out, barefoot, and followed me out onto the street. A neighbor's mail has been delivered to him accidentally, and he wanted to get it back to them. We lingered on the street, talking a while, and then I left.

The fourth and final type of account I find to be widespread among art-ists is the relational account. Artists talk of the value of taking studios to be near other artists, developing relationships with near and far-flung col-laborators, donating time and other resources to other artists and art insti-tutions; they build and nurture art institutions both informal and formal. They often do so with little hope of economic returns, and highlight rela-tional returns with few regrets. Some might argue that such activities can be seen as market-building, and in fact, they are sometimes best understood that way, a sort of networking. Artists are aware of the potential economic returns of such activities, to the extent that they often bracket them from more "real" social life, from the kinds of relational practices in which they have found value. Gregory pointed to such false relationships and their problems: "Socializing definitely is its own skill. You *do* think about, OK, we have to go to this bar for this afterparty and the drinks are $24, but I'm totally going to go. That's more than I would want to spend but I have to be-cause I need to be around these people. And so, yeah, you are having a good time, but it is also like, it's pretty . . . it is what it is, you know?" Whereas the kinds of market-building sociality that Gregory points to are "schmoozing" or "networking" and are bracketed by artists themselves as distinct from those things to which they assign relational value, relational accounts aim instead toward (and often have) interpersonal, even communitarian, out-comes. Acknowledging that artists can hope for, recognize, and value such returns—even as they sometimes also schmooze—is central to understand-ing investments in artistic practice.

Recall Will Schaff and his struggle to keep Fort Foreclosure alive. Near the end of Will's online campaign, I decided to drive up to Rhode Island for a benefit concert—one of the offline fundraisers happening that month. Will is a member of a sprawling, raucous street band called the What Cheer? Brigade, and they closed the night. In the midst of a sweaty, laughing crowd of several hundred—six-year-olds and the elderly dancing alongside crust punks—he grabbed the microphone and shouted at the top of his lungs: "Come be a part of it! It's better when you're a part of it! And the more you're a part of it, the better it is!" Later, without his mask, he took the microphone again. His voice breaking, he apologized for asking for help. Someone in the dark yelled, "Don't apologize! We love you!" The assembled crowd roared.

Relational accounts point to a belief among artists that their practices are, at the very least, good for society and, at best, transformational.[6] Artists often invest in community as they invest in their artistic practice, and many returns are relational in form. Rosemary, who with a collaborator runs a large project that costs them $26,000 a year, summed up the relational impulse eloquently: "People used to say, 'Well, you guys must be *so* rich to do this!' And OK, I grew up poor, it is *real* money, but at the same time, other people who are like in the middle class or whatever spend that much on school tuition for their kid and nobody thinks twice about it." She argued against "the idea that this is somehow abnormal. Like, I think it should be as normal as paying $26,000 a year for your . . . instead of having a kid, we have our community."

Recall Alan's words above. The most commonly cited value among artists who used relational accounts was the widespread belief that artistic practice was a unique site for the development of meaningful relationships with particular qualities. Artists did not say simply that they made friends through artistic practice; rather, they told me about specific kinds of art-facilitated relationships—either between themselves and audiences or between viewers—and argued that relationships developed through artistic practice were uniquely supportive, generative, and creative.[7]

Iris touched on this theme often during our interview. Her story started like anyone's: she had friends, she liked them. But it became clear with time that her artistic friendships had specific qualities. Her art career began when, as an unhappy pediatrician at the top of the hierarchy in her hospital, she went to what she called a "12-step" group for artists: "You name your art form in that group. And I almost choked trying to say that I was a writer. I mean, that's how I identified, that was more what I did at that point that was artistic. And I could barely choke out the word." Thanks to the group, she became comfortable calling herself an artist: "My identity as an artist grew up in that group; there was peer support for identifying as an artist." She told me about her friends, and about the particular qualities that friendships with other artists can hold: "We turn out for each other." Iris was still describing friendships like any others—but then I asked what a good day would look like, and she spoke more clearly about the specifics of artistic relationships: "A good day, I think, would be like Monday. One of the women in my writing group couldn't come on Monday, but the other one did, and we had a very nice collaboration in which we read to each other from our books; we talked about problems in the writing." Those conversations could be difficult: "There was something that we got talking about related to bringing out our writing to the world, and we were both in tears. I get what she's trying to do, and I can support her in that, and sort of explain her to herself. It was so rich and so valuable."

Relationships like these made art work—and artworks—possible for Iris and her colleagues. "It's like, I know I understand this woman's work, and what I'm saying to her will make it possible for this book to get finished, and for other people to have it." Later, we talked about an exhibition she had just opened. "That was a great day full of people that I care about, people that appreciate me and whom I appreciate. We support and encourage each other and care about each other." The relationships Iris talks about are normal relationships, plus a bit extra: they have contours that are specific to the arts, a combination of support and criticism and high expectations, and a shared value system. These relationships, many artists told me, have special and specific value.

Doug told me how tightly his artistic practice, the small business he ran together with his wife, and his personal relationships were twined together: "We've got a lot of clients we tend to work for, because, I think, we're most interested in helping people. I mean, I . . . interpersonal relationships are really, really important to me. More important to me than . . . I need to make enough money to, basically, pay for our mortgage. But, like, I really like meeting new people, and I really like to, like, help people." He told me about the work he did, and how central helping organizations to solve problems was to the meaning of his work: "I find that to be the most rewarding, because I feel like, you know, you do a lot of going in and helping people understand things, training them how to use things, getting tools, a lot of stuff where they can actually do it themselves. Training them how to do it, and then walking away. We find that to be really rewarding."

I asked Doug about how he ended up involved in a large exhibition he had been working on that would be opening soon, and he told me he knew the curator socially; they "go canoeing and bike riding and stuff." When he talked about the project, he didn't talk about its content or his own ideas, but about relationships with his collaborators: "I really just wanted to work with, again, a group of people, and have the people be, you know, part of the whole thing." Speaking about his own practice, he explained: "I tend to collaborate on things. Most of my art has been collaborative process stuff. Again, it's just kind of the kind of animal I am. I like to learn from other people, interact with other people. I'm not a person that's highly productive in a studio by myself. If I'm in a studio with somebody else, even if I'm working on my own stuff, I'm much more productive." Doug told the curator, " 'I'd like to find somebody else to work on this with me,' and he said, 'Well, do you know Samantha?' and I said no. And he said, 'Well, she's great.' "

At that point in the story, Doug broke off to ask me whether I had met her, whether I would like to, offered to put us in touch. When Doug and I had first spoken to make a plan to meet, our schedules were tight; he had less than an hour, he was about to mount a huge project, he had a meeting he had to be at. But then we met at a café, and when we ordered he chatted with the woman at the counter, asked if she didn't used to work there. She had, and they exchanged names. "Back from your big adventure?" he asked, and she nodded, told him she'd been in Korea for two years teaching English, and now she was back. They talked for a moment more, and then Doug and I sat outside and talked too long. When he finally acknowledged that he had to go, at least a half hour late for his next meeting, he was exceedingly friendly, suggested we meet again, said he wanted to know more about me, suggested grabbing lunch. I told him when I would be in town, promised to keep in touch, and he hustled off.

Back when Doug had broken off his story to tell me about Samantha, he used her full name; he did the same with everyone else he talked about. Many artists drop names, of course, but I noticed something when I talked to Doug: he didn't refer to people by name only when they were powerful, or interesting, or he thought I might know them. He wasn't name-dropping; he was giving the characters in his stories lives of their own, making connections, offering to let me see the cards in his mental Rolodex. When I realized this, I looked back at a number of transcripts, and found that artists using relational narratives did this constantly. Mark, for example, always used first and last names when he talked about people, whether they were the best-known potters in America or complete unknowns. He also took care to connect those people to each other throughout our conversations, pointing out who was whose teacher, who had once shared a studio. Artists who spoke this way talked about time in generations. They built bridges across time and space, and they welcomed me into their world, always asking if I'd be interested in meeting this person, if I might have time to go to see that one. Making connections between people seemed fundamental to their way of being, to their sense of a successful day or artwork or of a good life. Relationships, here, are not private pleasures; they are something more, and they are meant to be shared.

Some of the artists I spoke with told me they were beholden to the art world. It was their world, the basis of their relationships, of their very thoughts. These artists told me how all-encompassing relationships in the art world could be, how they colored everything. Adam, whose parents were artists, told me: "Having grown up in the art world, and these are the people I grew up around, the children of other artists and stuff, I just really became acutely aware that it really is my community. It really is my world." He stumbled a bit, looking for the right words. "It's impossible for me to think of things outside of that. That is my language. That is my reference point." He had been given a gift, but also an obligation: "I feel a responsibility to it somehow, as a member of it. And I am fortunate in the sense that I have gone through the art world since I was born. Always around other artists. My dad's friends and other people, friends of my mother's. I feel like I have a role and responsibility to fulfill it."

Many artists saw teaching in some form as a crucial strategy for both participating in and enabling a larger conversation, whether transnational and art historical or local and more closely bound to the soil. Mark had worked with a local cultural center to build their studios and develop ceramics programming, and had worked with the local tourism board to develop a potters' trail—a map of all the local artists, with information on their studios. He had no interest in a tenure-track job, and had recently turned down a very good position at a university out of state, but he did love teaching and had at the time of our interview forty private students. He acknowledged, in a quiet understatement, "I will say, I'm kind of interested in keeping the ceramic tradition alive around here."

Many artists told me they worked to build the community that they want feedback from; in many cases, such a community did not exist until they conjured it. Through investments in their own artistic practice, they feed forward to build the community from which they hope for feedback. Being in the conversation—participating in the art world, supporting other artists and being supported by others, engaging in critical and generative conversation—all of these things were highly valued by many of the artists I spoke with, and they were discussed at length by those who used relational accounts. Some valued such conversations so highly that they aimed to create structures and institutions to support them. Like Rosemary and her community, they imagined a better world, and worked to build it.

Some artists worked toward that better world through their artwork. Luis, a printmaker, has been making posters for forty years. He had trained in painting and drawing, but "because of the social movements, I got interested in the poster, what the poster does and how it functions. So I started making posters for different kinds of social movements." He described himself as being "in solidarity" with the movements he worked with, though he was not a member, strictly speaking: "I wasn't part of the farmworker union or anything, but I could identify with that struggle and what they went through." He drew on his family history when he explained his choices, saying it was an "easy" decision to start focusing on posters: "My parents were farm laborers. I mean, I grew up in farm labor camps." Later, he told me that if he had become the easel painter he was trained to be, he probably "would be doing it more as a hobby, as opposed to doing it professionally." As he spoke, it became clear why: "If it weren't for the fact that we have concerns about the world, and issues that need to be addressed, I wouldn't be as passionate about doing it. I would just be doing it for myself and my family." He compared that to the way he worked now: "It just gives it more validity for me, that it's actually doing something, more than just trying to get it into a gallery and sell it." Within a few sentences he returned to his background. "Both of my parents had no education. They didn't even read and write. My mom can still not even write her name. I mean, we didn't have any literature or books in our house. My kids have all that. My grandkids have all that." He was quiet for a while. "It's about life, you know what I mean? It's about using your art in a community so that you really feel like you're living, like you're alive every day." His eyes teared up, and he started to choke a little, then apologized. "Poverty in this country can make you just kind of give up, you know? And I think with art you don't give up. Because it just keeps you engaged in life. And if you're not engaged, then you give up." His artwork wasn't his only method of making the world a better place. But it was at the heart of everything he did.

Derrek, a painter, told me—and showed me—the world he aimed to build. During our interview he referred a few times to the gallery he had run for several years. I asked why it had closed, and he said the economic pressures simply got to be too much: "I mean, basically I was *paying* to show people's artwork." At the time, he was struggling to get by, and he spelled out the gallery's costs: "I think my biggest expense was $20 to touch up the paint on the walls and name tags. And that was a struggle; I had to miss a couple of meals to print name tags out. For someone else's show." He talked about his gallery as though it were a youthful indiscretion, but later in the interview he told me he was finalizing plans for a local art magazine he was hoping to begin publishing soon. Despite his earlier struggles, he hadn't turned away from the sort of DIY institution-building that I saw among many of those who drew on relational frameworks in their accounts. After I turned off my audio recorder, we talked about the town where he lives. He believed in it; told me about all of the places being rebuilt, who had bought the buildings, what they were doing. He asked if I wanted to see his new place, and we closed up the gallery where we'd met and walked the two blocks to an enormous building he had just rented. It was a huge space, half-built, raw and a bit dangerous, and he had plans for it. He said he wanted to make it the "Bauhaus of the South," have studios and live/work spaces for locals and people who would come to do residencies. I assumed he meant someday far in the future, but then he said he would be moving in along with the first studiomates later that month. He showed me around: three floors, a huge balcony. He didn't really have the tools he needed, had been holding hundred-pound walls up himself as he hammered them in. He showed me the garage; a friend had a fifteen-foot bar he could put out there along with some kegs. It would be a nice place, a good place to be.

Relational accounts share some features with vocational accounts, and like vocational accounts, they depart in meaningful ways from both pecuniary and credentialing accounts. Relational accounts of investment and return transcend clock time, displaying instead both task-oriented and generational understandings of time. Numerical and calculative justifications do not appear, and in these value-rational accounts the relevant market is unclear, though the institutional foundation is not—in relational accounts, the presence and structure of the liberal state is often apparent.[8] These accounts are rarely legible as explanations for investments to those outside the field, though, like vocational accounts, they involve widely shared meanings within the field of art and are usually understood there. They are strongly rooted in art worlds but oriented to a wide public; the ideal space for these accounts is public space, and the ideal artwork is one that sparks public debate.

.   .   .

Discomfort with the strictures of art as occupation takes active form in diverse accounts of the value of artistic practice, divergent valuations of that practice, and arguments about appropriate bases of value in the arts. These accounts, valuations, and arguments give form to conflicts between traditional and occupational practice. In the field of art, these conflicts are decidedly not between premarket "values" and monetary value. Artistic practice and the objects that often result were well commodified before the occupational turn, and within the field diverse values have long coexisted with market value, each mediating and modifying the other. Instead, conflicts over value in the art field today take the form of the insistence that specific bases of value in the arts be included in calculations of worth. These arguments point not to processes of decommodification (removal), but rather to processes of disagreement and of revaluation. Vocational accounts, for example, do not aim to make artistic practice priceless; rather, they are used to mediate pricing, *either* upward or downward depending on their deployment. Through arguments around the inclusion and exclusion of specific bases of value in the valuation of artistic practice, artists negotiate the conflicts between traditional and occupational practice. Some such accounts remain individual-level phenomena, while others resonate within the community and become widely shared meanings, deployed regularly.

Pecuniary and credentialing accounts are ways to make sense of investments in artistic practice in instrumentally rational, economically calculative terms; vocational and relational accounts allow artists to make sense of artmaking in evaluative terms. No one I spoke with used only one type of account to the exclusion of others in their conversations with me. Different practices are accounted for in different ways. Each framework mediates the other frameworks, and each has boundaries: too much emphasis on credentialing, for example, is undeniably taboo, and artists use idiosyncratic and nonmarket variables to minimize the appearance of calculation inherent in pecuniary accounts. But some artists I met did speak largely in terms of one type of account or another; their narratives were not pure, of course, but for some artists the balance of their accounts was heavily skewed in one direction or another.

My data suggest that artists skewing strongly in the direction of either pecuniary or credentialing accounts can build up a repertoire of framework-relevant skills and commitments and thus may follow somewhat path-dependent trajectories. As I suggest above, pecuniary frameworks for thinking about returns on investment allow risk to be relatively calculable; enable legible, occupational forms of artistic practice; and likely push artists toward sales careers. Credentialing, too, points toward art-related jobs and involves somewhat calculable risk, but its career outcomes are usually different; artists may be more likely to land in teaching and commercial work than to eventually make a living with sales. Both of these frameworks allow for the commensuration of the value of artistic practice with market value, but they do so in different ways, and may be associated with divergent outcomes. Looking to artists' demands for remuneration suggests one such varied outcome.

Artists using pecuniary accounts were likely, when they talked about remuneration, to refer to the objects they produced, even when those objects
were immaterial, and to talk about them within a logic of property. They
were likely to want to protect their rights over such objects. We see pecuniary accounts at play when artists ask for resale rights, exhibition rights, or
royalties for the use of their work. But not all artists ask for these rights, and
not all find them appropriate. Some artists—even some of those who make
and sell objects—account for the value of artistic practice using credentialing
frameworks, and they were more likely than other artists to imagine themselves to be service providers or professionals. These artists may calculate
the value of an object with more attention to an imagined hourly wage, and
they were more likely to talk about stipends, wages, and salaries. They might
ask not for resale rights but for clear contracts with institutions they see as
employers—the same institutions that artists using pecuniary frameworks
think of as purchasers or middlemen. Pecuniary and credentialing frameworks are both routes to commensuration of the value of artistic practice
with market value, but they are separate routes, leading to commensurations
with meaningful differences.

Artists who lean heavily on vocational and relational accounts do often
ignore market valuation to the extent possible. Artists I spoke with who
turned to these evaluative frameworks had access to a deep trove of rich,
legible accounts of the investments they make in their artistic practice that
do not gesture toward market valuation. But none of them avoided such
valuation at all times, and many did embrace economic calculations of the
value of artistic practice and instrumental rationality. These artists often carried out economic calculations in ways that pointed not to market value that
they might benefit from individually but to civic and social value. Vocational forms that lean on assumptions of the centrality of meaningful work
were associated, among artists I spoke with, with work in the nonprofit sector and especially in the arts field, while the relational account type shows
even more clearly how those accounting for the value of the things that they
do move resolutely away from market valuation. Understanding evaluative
frameworks and, in particular, relational accounts can help us to understand
the ways that artists account for investments in their practices so as to simultaneously minimize the legitimacy of market value and point to social

value. These artists were likely to view themselves as fundamentally "non-profit," and when they did build formal institutions they generally obtained nonprofit legal status for them. The artists I spoke with who used relational accounts viewed direct and indirect government support of the arts, including the benefits of nonprofit status, as both natural and appropriate. Battles over nonprofit status and other state subsidies generally derive from what artists see as a misunderstanding of the real value of the things that they do.

The subsidies represented by state money for the arts, direct stipends and prizes, art school tuition, nonprofit status, and other supports were rarely discussed by artists using pecuniary or credentialing frameworks or vocational accounts. They drew instead on relational logic when they promoted and defended subsidies, often positioning themselves as building cohesive, progressive, well-read, and active communities. Whereas economic analyses of the arts used to bolster subsidies focus in part on such relational activities by pointing to innovation and gentrification, artists themselves don't lean on such economic gains, and generally find them problematic and sometimes politically repugnant. They turn instead to civic returns, and argue that it is because the value of artistic practice can be found in the social that artistic practice deserves support. Artists' practices, in this view, help to build civil society, and though one can, of course, put a price tag on literacy and health along with imagination, creativity, and criticality, the artists I spoke with remind us through their use of relational frameworks that such social values are not at heart oriented toward the market; that their value lives elsewhere.

Alan told me about his discomfort with overarching discussions of remuneration and value in the arts, and acknowledged a flaw in generalized plans for artists' pay: "Anything I do on the street, that I'm just kind of playing and tinkering and doing stuff, I don't expect to get paid for that." He laughed: it's hard to admit that the reason you haven't signed up for the artists' union is that you don't even believe that much of your own hard work is worth a wage. But this position is widely held. Henry, thousands of miles away, told me almost the exact same thing: "I've had discussions with one friend, we've argued about this kind of thing, because I'm just interested in doing the stuff. This is what I want to do, and I do everything I can to make it happen." His friend did not agree: "He is really adamant about people understanding the importance of artists' work, that they should be supported, that it's worth money . . . just like, you would support your plumber, which I understand." But as Henry saw it, there were significant downsides to that kind of thinking: his friend "was working to support himself as an artist on his work. He does a lot of stained glass stuff. I'm like, well, you know, I fully agree with you, but I don't want any part of it. I see the other pitfall, of people calling themselves an artist and wanting money, and their work is crap. It's just, in the end, I just kind of want to do what I want to do."

Understanding how artists employ vocational and relational accounts can help the analyst to see how calculability is mediated, amplified, and impeded in accounts of value, as well as how pecuniary and credentialing frameworks can moderate uses of evaluative frameworks. If we look to the interplay of pecuniary, credentialing, vocational, and relational accounts, we can better understand artists' investments in artistic practice and the returns they expect. The next chapter looks specifically to the interactions between apparently contradictory accounts to understand how artists both align their practices with market valuation and retract their practices from market relations. While some artists—relatively few—do reject market relations entirely, most embrace calculability to account for at least a portion of their artistic practice. But the conflicts found in occupationalized practice, implied by the presence of vocational and relational frameworks, are always present, and for some they are crucially important.

.   .   .

Many potential bases of value and types of account are plausible and technically feasible, even within a single field. What explains the prominence of some, the absence of others? Within the field of the arts, those bases of value that draw heavily on contemporary visions of traditional practice are most likely to achieve widespread resonance and become widely shared meanings.

It is contemporary ideas about traditional practice that hold sway, regardless of the true landscape of historical practice. Some traditional practices and values, invisible to contemporary practitioners because they "make no sense," are preselected out of meaningful influence. While perhaps an infinite number of bases of value can plausibly account for a given practice, without a strong relationship to traditional practice (or, at least, contemporary visions of traditional practice) even plausible bases of value are unlikely to achieve widespread resonance among a community of practitioners, or to encourage social action. Remnants of not-yet-dead traditions create spaces of conflict where both old modes of valuation and new accounts of value can resonate and can become widely held, widespread meanings.

Accounts of value that lack the support of traditional imaginaries are difficult to sustain, and such potential accounts are unlikely to become widespread. Thus, despite the plausible viability of other types of account, vocational and relational accounts—the two evaluative types discussed in this chapter—dominate contemporary artists' conflicts over the valuation of their practices. Both draw on and fit within contemporary imaginaries of traditional practice—the art-for-art's-sake garret dweller and the local artisan whose studio serves as a community hub and speaks for the nation—and are therefore culturally legible within the field. These two types of account are used to minimize, moderate, and criticize pecuniary and credentialing accounts in artists' narratives of the value of artistic practice.

Other accounts appear or even recur, but fail to achieve significant traction. A look at arguments over remuneration in the arts allows us to see a few such proposals—negative cases that can illuminate the key role of subcultural resonance in the development of new accounts of value. Artists occasionally point towards others working in arts institutions (sometimes curators but more often security guards and secretaries) or, further afield, toward people in other careers (plumbers, lawyers) to argue that, like these others, artists work many hours a week, or that, like lawyers and other professionals, artists are highly credentialed.[9] Despite the occasional recurrence of entirely plausible arguments such as these (artists do work many hours, and such effort could be the basis of value; artists are often highly trained, and that too could be incorporated in the valuation of practice), they have not come to be widely shared meanings in the art community, and are very rarely used by artists in accounting for the value of their own practice. In my interviews, I have not heard them used at all, and they are a vanishingly small minority of the accounts I see in archival data. This type of account does not resonate with artists, and this lack of resonance can be explained by looking to artists' understandings of traditional practice—in particular, a belief that quality has never been based on hours worked, and a strong belief that artistic practice has always been in crucial ways singular, *not* just like any other job.

Relational accounts, only recently widespread and legitimated in the art field, are probably the least broadly convincing. Lofty assumptions about artists' intentions, often drawn from the writings not of artists themselves but of critics and curators, are readily deployed within the field as arguments against the value of particular sorts of practices and specific artworks, as in Claire Bishop's well-known piece of critical writing concerning "relational art work": "All relations that permit 'dialogue' are automatically assumed to be democratic and therefore good. But what does 'democracy' really mean in this context?" Bishop discusses the artist at hand, and says that his "intervention is considered good because it permits networking among a group of art dealers and like-minded art lovers, and because it evokes the atmosphere of a late-night bar. Everyone has a common interest in art, and the result is art-world gossip, exhibition reviews, and flirtation. Such communication is fine to an extent, but it is not in and of itself emblematic of 'democracy.'" Continuing along this vein, she writes that the artist's "microtopia gives up on the idea of transformation in public culture and reduces its scope to the pleasures of a private group who identify with one another as gallery-goers."[10] The caricatures that define the outer limits of relational accounts of value are less well known outside the art field than those that mark the outer limits of pecuniary, credentialing, and vocational accounts, as I discuss in the next chapter. But along with the others they serve as archetypical cautionary tales, shaping our understanding of appropriate goals, behavior, and accounts within the art community.

So, if relational accounts can seem unbelievable even to insiders, how do they become widespread, even institutionalized? In the arts, both organic elites and collective movements propose historical and theoretical support for accounts of value, disseminate accounts and arguments, and help accounts to become widely shared meanings. Elites (well-known artists, art professors in well-regarded MFA programs, some art critics) influence contemporary understandings of traditional practice through their practice, through their written work and works written about them, and through teaching, and can promote particular individual bases of value over others. Relational value was legitimized beginning in the 1990s in the emergence of "new genre public art" and "relational aesthetics," as art historians theorized about and promoted specific artists and their work.[11] Such writings disseminated ideas widely, and often assumed the authority to "speak for" artists. One critic wrote that art should move "toward sharing power rather than imposing solutions, toward healing wounds inflicted by the fragmentation and social segregation of contemporary public space."[12] One artist wrote that "new genre public art" consisted of a "fluid and broad range of practices which aim at social change and raising consciousness. Artists share their practice in collaboration with groups of non-artists (or non-professional artists) in such a way as to provide, among other things, a transformative experience."[13]

Elites interact with and sometimes inspire the collectives (artists' unions and other groups) that have aimed to speak for artists generally, and have promoted specific bases of value widely when they speak to issues of remuneration. Relational accounts of the value of artistic practice pose new problems for such organizations, which have long envisioned artists as object-makers and worked to protect their rights to physical and intellectual property. However, by combining relational accounts (with their common-good assumptions) with credentialing logics, collective movements have been able to create and promote new arguments for artists' remuneration.

Collective movements can appear to create "new" meanings when they argue before a wide audience unfamiliar with the communities and elites that are the movement actors, and can influence structural changes in the valuation of the arts through pressure on relevant state and institutional structures. Elites too have structural capacities that allow them to bring previously obscure meanings shared only by a few to a wide audience, and can contribute to the institutionalization of accounts both by lending support to collective movements and by building institutions themselves—witness, for example, the rise and spread of MFA and PhD programs (with their attendant funding, credibility, and credentials) in social practice, new genre public art, and relational aesthetics. Today, one school offers "contextual practice" as an area of concentration within its MFA degree; the curriculum "supports students in the production of socially engaged art projects that respond to or catalyze public contexts and audiences."[14] Another school of fine arts offers a concentration in "social practices," explaining that "artists working within [social practice] either choose to co-create their work with a specific audience or propose critical interventions within existing social systems that inspire debate or catalyze social exchange."[15] Each of these recently developed programs was spearheaded by an individual or small group of elite practitioners, and through cohorts of students, what was quite recently a "new" meaning has become a widely shared account of the value of artistic practice.

The cracks between the structures of traditional and professional practice do not only allow remnants of the meanings of traditional practice to leak through into contemporary rhetoric, they also leave room for the development and resonance of new accounts. The revaluations discussed here create and exploit disjunctures as openings for new pathways to value.[16]

· · ·

It's clearly not as simple as "love or money." Artists have access to diverse claims both when they talk love *and* when they talk money, and those distinct accounts of value dance together better than we might have imagined.

Commensuration is the unwieldy term used by economic sociologists to refer to the social processes by which multiple parties come to agree on value.[17] An entire subfield in economics, cost-benefit analysis, concerns itself with such sticky issues as the dollar value of human life, a beautiful shoreline, air that doesn't trouble your lungs. While the goal in that field is most often a dollar value that all parties will accept, economic sociologists look instead at the ways each party reaches such a dollar value and multiple parties negotiate their way to agreement, and the ways we come to believe that a dollar value is appropriate at all. Imagine a scale—the old-fashioned two-pan balance we use as the symbol for justice. Social studies of commensuration ask how we calibrate that scale, how we come to balance it, and why that point of balance varies so strongly by time and place. Pricing an artwork and putting a dollar value on your time are uses of that scale—you're using the common metric of the dollar to assert value. Put very simply, when we talk about commensuration we talk about processes of agreement about value.[18]

We continue to see resistance to economic commensuration—both to agreements made and to the validity of the dollar as final yardstick—in everyday life. We see it in battles over wages and pay rates, over the value of a landscape or a life. Might we usefully imagine such resistance as something like a process? Is it possible that our attention to commensuration—agreement—and its qualities in surprising arenas may have led us to forget, ignore, or deny its opposite? We have a wealth of research from economics and sociology informing our understanding of processes of commensuration, but social studies of commensuration most often treat the opposite of these processes as simply a null hypothesis unworthy of sustained attention. I argue, in contrast, that commensuration's opposite is not a simple lack of commensuration (what might be called incommensuration), but an active process, one just as likely to lead to patterned and distinct processes and divergent outcomes as the processes of agreement we have grown to regard as central to understanding valuation: something more like *de*commensuration.

In the past three chapters, I have sketched a model of such a social process of disagreement about value in working life. I suggest that such processes consist of three stages: first, as traditional practices undergo an occupational turn, tensions between old and new orders of worth come to be expressed in conflicts over valuation. Second, diverse accounts of value proliferate. Third and finally, some accounts—those that draw on contemporary visions of traditional practice—achieve widespread resonance and become widely shared meanings through field-specific institutionalization mechanisms. In this process of disagreement, commensurations are undone and made anew; quantities are transformed back into qualities, and we are forced to reconsider the value of artistic practice.[19] To return to the case at hand: artists draw a landscape of value that they traverse themselves. But a question remains: how do artists use these diverse and often apparently logically inconsistent accounts together, how do they move within the map they have drawn—and why do they bother?

This Way Be Monsters   5

ELAINE IS A PHOTOGRAPHER, CHOREOGRAPHER, AND DANCER. For twenty years, her day job was in accounting, but at the time of our interview, thanks to a prestigious fellowship awarded as a lump sum, she had been able to leave her job and focus only on her work. We met at a hip, dark-paneled supper club and shouted over the music. I asked her what was involved in mounting a performance, and her calculating self, armed with the newest version of Excel, shone through as she told me about the costs of the work—though always with an undercurrent of something beyond the pecuniary. She told me about a commission she had received the previous year, saying, "They paid me to do that, and it wasn't a lot of money. I got $2000. The lighting technician came with it, so I didn't have to hire a lighting designer. We had to pay for postcard design. I took the photos; I didn't have to pay a photographer." The piece involved eleven performers: "I paid everybody the same wage, ten bucks an hour for rehearsal, and then I had to also rent a rehearsal space. Luckily, I have a friend who has a studio that he lets me rent for really cheap, so he rented it to me for five dollars an hour." She was on top of the budget, at least early on, keeping a spreadsheet of each rehearsal, "who was there, kept track of how much they were gonna get, and just kept a running tally."

Elaine was able to minimize costs in a few different ways. "I pretty much did all of the costumes, either out of my own stuff or sourcing stuff myself, or what people had, what people were willing to wear. So didn't spend a whole lot on costumes." But her dancers ate up a huge chunk of the budget: "I just paid everybody their hourly wage through the whole . . . usually right before you have a show, there's a long tech week, where you're in the theater a lot, and so I paid everybody their hourly wage for that." Pecuniary logics clearly structure this narrative—witness the easy use of numbers and the many references to calculations (even, unusually, to a spreadsheet), and the clear references to clock time, to rental costs and wages calculated by the hour. Even here, though, occasional flashes of other values occasionally surface. "Luck" is everywhere; later, as she continued to tell me about the show, she said that someone very "graciously" did some work for her at a discount. We continued to talk about the project, and it became clear that vocational demands steered Elaine's calculations away from a strict bread-and-butter accounting, no matter how readily she could tally her costs. Her goal, as we shall see, was not to come out ahead or even to break even on the performance, but to complete the work, and to complete it with her ethics and vision intact.

Elaine was awarded $2000 for the commission, an amount that, she said, "sounds like a lot of money" but which ended up being less than half of what she spent on the piece. When she told me about paying her dancers, it was apparent both that if she wanted to come in under budget she could have planned the piece differently and that her hourly rate is set through a mix of ethical and financial pressures. "I, for whatever reason, ended up working with a huge cast, and so that involves . . . Not everybody does it this way but, um, in an ideal world, you pay your performers for rehearsals. I can't speak for theater or for other choreographers, but it's really, it's a nice, you want to do that. That's the right thing to do, is pay people." She stumbled a moment, then continued: "Usually, you just pay an hourly wage, so I pay people ten bucks an hour, which, in the real world, is nothing, but . . . unfortunately, for dance, around here, that seems to be sort of average, or on the higher side, which is . . . unfortunate." She laughed dourly. "I paid myself an hourly wage for rehearsal but that doesn't even touch on . . . I didn't keep track of preparatory time, which is lame, I should've done that. So, over that, not counting the choreographic fee, I think I went over budget by, like, $2500, probably. Which, luckily, I had a full-time job that I could subsidize it with, and ah . . . and I did!"

When Elaine told me about these decisions, her voice was no longer the confident tone of the accountant; she hemmed and hawed, nodded to the absurdities of some of her choices, laughed at herself. Things simply happened, "for whatever reason." She acknowledged a crucial point only in passing: when she said that she "didn't keep track of preparatory time" and that she went over the budget even "not counting the choreographic fee," she meant that drawing an income from the commission was her lowest priority. She used up the commission she was awarded and then spent out of pocket to create the work she envisioned, one where aesthetic demands took priority and ethical concerns drove a significant part of the budget. But she did not keep track of or prioritize her own pay, which, by any calculation, should have been by far the largest cost of producing the work because she acted as the creator, choreographer, director, videographer, and producer. *Not including* these significant but unaccounted-for costs, she came out of the project very pleased and $2500 in the hole.

Elaine interwove pecuniary and vocational accounts within one narrative, and this interplay between the two types of account is central to her story of the decisions she made. Occasionally, she nodded to apparent conflicts between the two types of account, but did not accept such conflict as insurmountable. Rather, the push and pull of pecuniary and vocational accounts is central to her understanding of this practice as "her work."

Making money at her art—even making a living at it—sometimes appears central to Elaine's self-understanding as a "real" artist; when we met, the first thing we talked about was how, thanks to the large fellowship she had just won, she was finally comfortable identifying as what she called a "working artist." But it was clear later in our interview, when she contrasted her work to what she called "dance jobs," that making a living wasn't all that mattered in that definition: "I have just done a couple of jobs that are dance jobs, like choreographic jobs that I got paid for. Little freelance gigs that were interesting, but they weren't exactly . . ." She looked for the right words. "I found them interesting to do, and yet, they were sort of limiting, in that it was sort of thrown together, and it isn't my perfect setting, and . . . you feel a bit compromised, and it feels a little bit like you're dumbing down your work so it's more accessible." Doing dance jobs, then, couldn't be counted as part of her own work: "That's in my field, and I enjoyed doing it, and yet . . . I don't know how satisfying that would be, to do that all the time."

In the arts, art work and commercial work can be nearly indistinguish-able—both the process and the outcome of a "job" can look to an outsider like an artist's "work," but artists themselves usually draw sharp lines be-tween the two. Artists like Elaine weave apparently incompatible accounts together into coherent narratives that are used to understand, assert, and promote value in a specifically artistic context.

. . .

While some artists' accounts skew heavily toward one or another basis of value, the majority do not. When a single account isn't balanced with others, it can devolve into caricature. As I have remarked earlier, people say artists don't talk about money. When they say that, they have a particular carica-ture in mind: the artist-as-speculator, an art accounted for only in pecuniary terms: an artist with a clear sense of the risks of art practice and a strategy for maximizing returns on investment. It's this image of the artist that we're talking about when we say that talking money is taboo in the arts: the profit-maximizing artist playing the art game, bending to its rules, trying only to make a living.

The soulless artist as speculator is only one of the caricatures stand-ing at the boundary of the meaningful world of art practice. Vocational-ism, too, has its limits: the artist who works only "for love, not money," always independently wealthy or garret-poor, represents within the art world an unfair advantage either in patrimony or willingness to suffer. The Sunday painter—in this telling, often "retired," with a wink, since she never worked—represents how far out of touch and out of step those who make art only for leisure can be with the rest of the community. Too much emphasis on credentialing is undeniably taboo; artists delegitimize prac-tices they see as aiming toward commercial work or the tenure file, artists who do "the same old stuff over and over again," who make artwork only to "keep up their credentials." Relational accounts have been only recently widespread and legitimated in the art field and appear to be the least se-cure. The caricatures that define the outer limits of relational accounts of value—the drunken men who simply aim to legitimate hanging out at the bar, the "politically active" young artist who fundamentally misunderstands the disadvantaged populations she uses in her practice, or the artist who points to dialogue with a "public" made up only of close friends—are, as discussed above, relatively new, and less well known outside the art field than the other caricatures. But all of these caricatures live in the minds of most artists and structure their narratives and their criticisms.

Understanding how particular frameworks coexist alongside others allows us to see why these caricatures are both meaningful and absent from the real world of arts practice. Artists may once have performed an interest in disinterestedness to climb the status ladder in a bipolar art field, but today's art worlds are far more multivalent.[1] Caricatures define the unacceptable upper limit of each account of value; the scheming artist-as-speculator and others shape artists' narratives even though these caricatures cannot be seen to populate the real world. These caricatures are meaningful "types" of artists, and though no individual artist fits any one profile, these archetypes define the boundaries of the world of contemporary art practice. Each marks the outer limit of one route to the valuation of practice; continue down this path, these caricatures tell us, and you are no longer an artist. This way be monsters.

.   .   .

Midway through the research for this book I sorted my bits of paper into piles and looked to answer what I imagined would be a simple question: which types of account co-occur with one another most often, and which co-occur rarely? As before, I looked to narratives of investment: stories with a beginning and an end that involved resource commitments and returns on those investments. While some such narratives seemed to utilize only one logic, one type of account, others involved more complex relationships between diverse frameworks, as when Elaine wove pecuniary and vocational logics into her story of a single project. Artists sometimes seemed to contradict themselves; they told me stories from one perspective, then jumped to another standpoint midway through. No single narrative contained all four types of account, but narratives—even single sentences—that used two or three types of account were not uncommon.

When I started to consider whether artists would use pecuniary accounts together with credentialing, vocational, or relational accounts more often, it seemed clear to me that pecuniary and credentialing accounts were reasonably compatible. They struck me as two sides of the same rational coin, and I expected to find many narratives where pecuniary and credentialing accounts wove in and out of one another easily. After all, credentialing can be understood as an economically rational practice, falling together with pecuniary accounts under the umbrella of a Weberian instrumental rationality. Since they seemed logically compatible, I expected to see the two types of account co-occurring often within narratives of investment. Perhaps, as the analyst, I would be able to collapse the two into one category; I looked forward to the parsimony of a single instrumentally rational category of accounts.

When I looked to the narratives I had collected and analyzed, one tiny pile immediately made sense: as I had expected, pecuniary and relational accounts, distant cousins, were almost never used in concert. But I also found very little overlap between pecuniary and credentialing accounts, despite their ideal logical coherence. The few accounts in that pile gestured occasionally at the ways a sale might both pay one's rent and help to build a reputation if the buyer was right—but this didn't happen often. The third pile, a high stack of short and long stories, sliding about on the desk, surprised me.

Pecuniary and vocational accounts are, of the four types discussed in the previous chapters, most commonly used in concert, despite their apparent logical incoherence. Recall, for example, how pecuniary accounts are short-term and specific, while vocational accounts call on transcendent, suspended notions of time; recall how often numerical justifications appear in pecuniary calculations, while numbers are banished from the world of vocational accounts. That these two types of account are used together so often may appear strange to the analyst who expects to hear logically coherent accounts—but not to anyone who has spent time in art communities, where the push-pull of love and money is central to arts practice and has been for some time. In art worlds, the space around and between "doing it for money" and "doing it for love" is one made specially to fit a dance whose steps we all know, for which we improvise our own flourishes.

Recall Elaine's sense that her "dance jobs" were "just" jobs, how different they felt from her "own work." Other artists, too, are often very aware of this element of a given artwork's provenance and openly devalue work they see as oriented toward sales or fees as "commercial," showing that vocational intent matters even in the work's reception. Further complicating the issue, feelings can change, and what was at one point rewarding as creative work can come to be seen as "just a job" and not an element of one's creative practice. Sophie started making screen prints that she sold for a time, but after they became very popular she began to feel as though they were no longer "her work." When it started, she said, "I just had a few ideas and I started making posters that were not commissioned and selling them through a small publishing house. They were like, 'We like this, we'd sell it in our shop, bring it in,' and I did." The prints sold out in a week, and the shop asked for more; in time, other stores started carrying them as well, and Sophie started to lose interest: "It became, weirdly, something outside of me. I didn't have control. It was like [she threw up her hands], 'Oh, this is happening.'" I asked whether she still made them, and she smiled ruefully. "Yes. Very much so. I do a lot of order fulfilment." She laughed, and told me that the prints might be the first thing browsers would find if they googled her name, which she found "interesting, and maybe confusing." She told me she "keeps the practices pretty separate," and that any sense that the prints were "her work" was long gone: "I make those now as a source of bread-and-butter income. It's not my creative outlet. It doesn't feel like I really need to make them, whereas there are other pieces where I feel like, 'Oh, I *want* to make this and see what happens.'"

Adonis told a similar story when I asked about his work assisting another artist. He said, "It didn't always feel like work. When I wasn't making as much of my own work, making work for him felt like my release, like my creative energies were being poured into that." When he started spending more time on his own work, his assisting work wasn't as meaningful anymore: "Working as an assistant just became a regimented, I'm here 9:30 to 5:30, Monday through Thursday thing. And that started to feel like work." His assisting job felt like creative work, but then suddenly his situation changed, and his job—about which very little changed—was all at once something he experienced as "regimented." Understanding the interplay of pecuniary and vocational accounts can allow us to see how, even for artists entirely committed to making a living at art, the high valuation of the ability to do one's "own work" rather than just "jobs" alters the math involved in pecuniary calculations. Elaine and the other artists discussed in this chapter use pecuniary and vocational accounts in concert to position themselves, their practices, and their works as both serious and called—as doing it for love *and* money.

· · ·

One strategy for bringing pecuniary and vocational logics together is to claim that the economics of the art field are not well understood by neoclassical economics. Artists regularly claim that art pricing is just crazy, suggest that speculators and tire kickers screw up what might otherwise be normal pricing mechanisms, and point to ridiculously low or high fees to argue that, here, economic logic just doesn't apply in the usual sense. Crazy money and a funny economy bring pecuniary and vocational accounts into concert.

John, like many, pointed to a particular work when he told me that art pricing was completely detached from labor and material costs or other, more everyday bases of value. He told me about a Chelsea gallery show he had seen: "It was, like, those plastic little pint containers for strawberries stacked up in a pyramid. The thing was going for $12,000 or something like that." He laughed, then compared the price tag on the pint containers to the $6,000 he had recently received for a commissioned public sculpture, one that cost nearly that amount to produce, and shook his head. "I mean, if that whole thing went for $6,000 and somebody else can stack a bunch of plastic containers up for $12,000, that's in a different price category. That's a whole different ballgame."

Josh told me that the sale of his work had little to do with its qualities, and distanced himself from the value he created in the art market: "I was spending money on my work that was paying itself back. That was breaking even, which was like, $50,000 a body of work, $40,000 a body of work, so that cycle was happening, and that has everything to do with the market, not me." Carlton, too, told me that prices had little to do with the qualities of the objects he produces, and he prefers not to try to make sense of them: "Pricing has almost nothing to do with what I think. I feel like it's just totally not a part . . . it doesn't come to mind when I am making something, and I hope it never does." He went on to explain why: "It has so much to do with speculation and so much to do with what they think somebody will pay for a certain thing, or how to generate interest in a certain thing by making it cheaper or making it more expensive." Carlton is aware of the communicative properties of prices, and he prefers to hold them at arm's length.

Artists who point to the craziness of art world economics very often suggest that their own willingness to go without pay is excellent evidence of such craziness. Josh's prices are quite high, and one might imagine that when he told me about his prices he had been talking about his livelihood, that he drew an income from his work, but that was not the case. I asked him about his high prices and his household budget, and he said of his work: "It's very expensive. But I've never made money on it. I've never thought of my artwork as a means of independent wealth, *ever*. I've always recouped what it cost to make a project. I haven't always made significant gains on a project." Like Elaine, whose words opened this chapter, Josh spoke rationally in calculated terms about the investments necessary to produce his work and the returns he could expect based on past experience—but a closer look shows that neither artist pays themselves, choosing instead to follow their artistic vision, to *maybe* aim to break even.

Adam has maintained an art practice for many years alongside the small business he runs. Today he is represented by a gallery, but never "comes out ahead"—draws a personal income—from the practice. About this he exhibits no confusion whatsoever. "The art income probably doesn't quite pay for the art even now. It doesn't contribute to my family at all. No. In fact, not only does it not contribute . . . See, the problem is that I have to come up with x number of dollars every month just to support myself, pay for insurance, pay for the house. And the problem is that the art is a detriment." He explains how the math doesn't add up: "Even though I might get my expenses paid for by a school or a museum, or I might even sell a work, it just covers itself. So what happens is, let's say it takes two weeks of that month. If I'm supposed to come up with $25,000 every month, I'm not earning. I only have two weeks to come up with that $25,000 because the other two weeks I'm not making anything. I'm just covering the expenses that are additional." If the economics of the art world don't work as they should, in rational ways, and if the value of an artwork is not well explained by the features of that artwork, it becomes quite easy to combine pecuniary and vocational accounts into a seamless narrative—since it turns out the economics of the situation, the sorts of pecuniary accounting that we might assume could make sense, are not so straightforward after all. When artists point to the "crazy" economics of the art world, they suggest that pecuniary and vocational calculations might not, after all, be so incompatible in this context.

Some artists say the economics of the art world are just bonkers. Others, though, see those same economics as functioning perfectly well; they point instead to their own low or intentionally minimized economic goals, suggesting that a growth model is irrelevant to an artist's practice. As when artists insist that the economics of the art world are "bizarre," these accounts suggest ways that love and money might not be so incompatible after all. Peter, an adjunct professor at an elite art school married to another artist with a more stable job, had recently turned down a tenure-track position in another city when we spoke: "They didn't understand why I couldn't commute or whatnot, because it would have been great to have both paychecks, we totally could have done it. But I just . . . we don't need the extra money. She doesn't make a lot of money but it's enough to pay the bills." Like most artists, Peter and his partner didn't make nearly the money their two graduate degrees could demand, but they didn't aim to, either—though he referred to their lack of money as a problem both personally and creatively a number of times during our interview.

As I discussed in the introduction, almost all of the artists I spoke with intentionally earned less money than they potentially could have. Artists rarely price their artworks as high as they possibly could, hoping instead to balance the need for income with the hope for "right" kind of buyer, ethical and political concerns, and even aesthetic demands that consider the price an integral element of the work. The "bohemian" lifestyle artists are often seen to aim for and do often live doesn't, on close inspection, look much like our stereotype of it. Adonis, twenty-six at the time of our interview, told me that he "took a step to get a studio" in New York, two hours from home and his day job, together with his collaborator. When I asked what that involved, I found that it was more than a simple commitment of available finances: "We had a couple of prominent people in the art world become interested in the stuff we were doing, but they bailed on us, because we didn't have a studio in New York. And so we said, OK, well, if you're not coming to us, we will come to you." They signed a lease on a New York studio, though they couldn't really afford it. "We have become paupers. We sleep on the floor in our studio, and here we decided to share a bedroom, to cut our expenses down . . . It's a horrible situation. It's just cheap." Adonis would be more than happy to move away from his bohemian lifestyle; he simply feels that he is making investments necessary for his artistic practice, investments that he believes will pay off in the near future.

For a long time, Henry lived in a live / work space, a subsidized housing and studio arrangement often offered by cities trying to get a piece of the gentrification potential artists are assumed to bring with them. It may have looked cool to outsiders and was certainly a good deal by the square foot, but he hated it: "I had a live / work space for nine years, and I didn't like it. At all. But it was very cheap and it's what I could afford." I asked why he didn't like living there, and he clarified: "Sculpture, there's just a safety issue. You'd be sanding on something that was a carcinogen, and it's like, there's my . . . I can see my butter on my table." By the time of our interview, with more stable finances, he was paying much more for separate housing and studio space and was much happier, but saw the live / work space phase as a necessary evil in his career. For many older artists, especially those with families, bohemia tends to look a bit different, and to be less visible—it can even appear to be a bit luxurious. Artists move out of cities and to lower-cost areas; they buy larger houses than they otherwise might to have the space to work; they stay home with their children in a country where child care costs, especially for multiple children, easily dwarf incomes. A few left-leaning women I interviewed laughed at the ways that their life in grown-up bohemia now looked a lot like the America seen in 1950s television, staying home with the children and canning their own tomatoes. I stayed in the guesthouse of an artist whose incredibly beautiful home belied the time he had spent living first in a tent and then a shack on the property, the years spent building a relationship with the neighbors to enable the land's purchase, and the decades spent scrounging materials and hand-building the house himself. He wasn't the only one; a few months later, I visited the sprawling estate—gorgeous house, studio buildings, gallery, and sculpture garden—of another artist who had lived in a tent while he slowly built his home; when everything was swept away by Katrina a few years before we met, he and his family were back in that tent until he managed to rebuild. Bohemia today only rarely looks like the Left Bank image we all share, but artists persist in a wide-spread commitment to low-cost living.[2]

Many artists who don't make a living at art work told me that they could make art their job if they wanted to. Bodie, the graduate of an elite MFA program, told me that he had an "arrogant belief that if I wanted to make a very desirable artwork I could." He sighed, and explained: "Painters do really well. If you do work that looks a particular way, people are going to love it; it's going to be a hot little commodity." A skeptical analyst might assume that Bodie is just squeezing sour grapes—but in my research I spoke with several artists who did make the choices that others disparage as too sales-oriented, and the "arrogant belief" that Bodie refers to is not so arrogant after all. It is very feasible to make a living as an artist if you put a goal of sales above all others; it's only that very few artists do this. And when they do, if they don't get the balance just right, they risk being cast out of the fine art community, of falling on the wrong side of those caricature-sentries that guard the boundaries of legitimate art practice.

When Bodie and others tell me that they just don't care, don't really want to sell things, have other priorities that matter more, it seems to me not particularly radical to consider whether or not they might in fact be telling the truth. It is only if we see the purpose of art to be making a living by selling artworks that we assume he must be dishonest, fooling himself, a dupe. Envisioning the purpose of artmaking to be making a living at artmaking is, for the vast majority of artists, a ridiculous assumption. For most purposes, including the issues at hand here, we may want to trust Derrek's intuition, skill, and knowledge of his local market when he tells me, straightforwardly, "If I wanted to make an income, living in the South, I could paint crosses." There's no shame in garret life with a beret. If we can assume that at least a majority of artists could make a more profitable living if they aimed to, then we must acknowledge that their low economic goals might reflect a choice rather than a post hoc justification of a sad situation. Everyone gives something to their practice, and many of the things artists invest in their practices have ramifications well beyond present budgetary concerns. The artists I spoke with acknowledged the ways that the sacrifices they made to their artistic practice amounted to a not-for-profit economic model, and showed me how garret life, lived right, can be central to balancing love and money in the arts.

Some artists said that the economics of their field were crazy; others claimed the economics of their field made sense but they weren't the rational, maximizing actors of economic theory, so pecuniary and vocational frameworks could live in harmony. A third strategy was widespread among those who used pecuniary and vocational accounts in concert: claiming that either aesthetic goals or political, ethical, or personal self-actualization demanded primacy. These artists usually made this claim with a nod to the social dominance of pecuniary frameworks, just as women engaged in care work often acknowledge the social dominance of economic thinking before calling instead on alternative metrics of value.[3] They did not claim that pecuniary and vocational goals could mix; rather, they affirmed the distinction, even opposition between the two. These artists acknowledged that an undercurrent of pecuniary demands was always present—one has to eat, after all, to feed Derrek's many meters—but they showed how vocational logics took precedence whenever possible. Their uses of the two logics in concert simply flipped the socially dominant relationship between the two types of account, and claimed a new hierarchy of types—a happy marriage of unequal partners, one making all the rules.

Armando, as discussed earlier, told me several times that you just "can't" apply straightforward cost-benefit analysis to artistic practice if you're going to do what the piece demands of you; recall his $60 tubes of paint. When I asked him why he stopped keeping track of his painting time, he told me again that such accounting is incompatible with artistic practice: "I got really bad at that. When you're in it, you have to dive completely into it." Sophie told me that she had to work seventy hours a week at her day job because her work was expensive to make—as though it was entirely outside her discretion: "I worked, like, I don't know, sixty to seventy hours per week because I wanted to have enough money to take two months off to produce work for my own show. I knew that some of the work I was making for my own show was going to be expensive. So I wanted to have enough to do that, so I worked crazy hours."

The terms artists use when they speak of aesthetic demands—you "have to" do things, you "can't" accept limitations, things simply happen, outside of the artist's control—sometimes even assign agency to the artworks. Sean told me about the portraits he used to paint on commission, but said he'd stopped when he "decided to start indulging what I was interested in." When Carlton talked about making work he couldn't really afford to produce, the demands of the artworks were front and center: "Money stuff has always been a problem. When my work changed, I started to entertain these projects. I just started making these things that required me to buy certain kinds of materials that were more expensive than I was used to." When he left school, this became a pressing issue: "I was like, how can I even keep making the work that I want to make? Because it seemed to require certain materials that were just so expensive that I couldn't do it." He had "quite a bit of a crisis there for a while," since, of course, artworks can be made cheaply. But in the end, making cheaper work came with its own constraints: "It would put a limit, or it would change the way I was thinking about what I was doing and what I was doing would become about finances and about money." Notice the words Carlton used, words echoed in other artists' narratives when they combine pecuniary and vocational logics: the work "required" him to buy expensive materials; it started "going" in its own direction; he just had to "entertain" these new projects. In fact, doing less costly art would alter the content of his work—would make it "about finances and about money."

Some artists told me, over and over again, that they simply "had to" make art. It's just who I am; it's how I prefer to deal with and act in the world; I love it; I've already given it so much; it's all I'm good at. If we think of pecuniary accounts as closely tied, in many cases, to jobs—to doing it for money—then most of these specifications are not so out of step with the demands of working and professional life today. We're supposed to find ourselves in our working life, love our jobs, express our true selves through our work. Critics of neoliberalism and its personal demands have shown us for decades how tightly wedded these particular iterations of vocationalism are to today's ideal worker.[4] Recall Adam, who talked about how hard it was financially to take time away from his small business to engage in his art practice. I suggested that other artists might have quit under these circumstances, and he agreed: "I almost left the art world. Like, I got really close because I am a successful small business owner, and at some point I had to make a decision. Should I go ahead and just finally leave?" But his commitments to the art community trumped any thoughts of abandoning artistic practice for a simpler, less precarious life. The self-actualization these artists pointed to was one that was only possible through work—a highly occupationalized artistic practice—and so twined pecuniary and vocational accounts together in a tight braid.

.   .   .

Among the artists I spoke with who deployed pecuniary and vocational accounts within single narratives, three strategies were widespread—artists claimed that the economics of the art world were crazy, told me they had minimized their economic needs, and said that, barring death from starvation, self-actualization through artistic work would always win out. All of these were strategies used by artists to move seamlessly between pecuniary and vocational accounts of value, to engage in the dance between love and money so central to and generative in the field of artistic practice. One outcome of such strategies—the primary outcome of interest in this study—is an account that "makes sense," both to the artist speaking and the interlocutor. I wondered, though, whether there might be other, more instrumental outcomes of such combinations of accounts as well. Among those who used pecuniary accounts to the near exclusion of others, I had seen a tendency toward sales and an interest in property rights; among those who leaned heavily toward vocational accounts I had observed widespread experience in nonprofit employment. I wondered: what do those who regularly mix pecuniary and vocational accounts look like?

Looking at pricing suggests one concrete way that vocational accounts interact with pecuniary accounts. Armando taught art privately, and at first, he suggested that his prices were reasonable given the local context, but then immediately acknowledged that his reference group was the wrong one before explaining why his prices were so low: "I set my prices competitive to the other art schools in the area. Except because I'm individually teaching people, and it's not a group class effort, I think my prices at the time I started were a little bit lower than everybody else. I just raised my prices by, like, $1.25 a class, and that was the first time we've raised prices in the five years that we've been operating." He described his reasoning: "Tuition for eight weeks of classes went from 280 to 290, basically. And I don't want to go over $300. I don't want to do that. I probably could do it, and I would probably still have my same core of people, but I don't, I don't want art to be something that is only the bastion of people that are able to afford it. I don't want this to be just like a privileged arena." Armando's discussion of his ethical reasons for pricing his services so low is notable only in that it is relatively lengthy; more commonly, artists simply state such reasons for the choices they have made, without much explication.

Land is quite calculating in her approach to pricing, but finds room for a discount much of the time. I asked her for the "equation" she had mentioned, and she told me, "Kind of like how many hours I put into it. I have a list of hours that I put into my drawings, and I basically look at the clock, I start my drawing, and when I am done I look at how many hours I have been working on it. And then I multiply it by what I think I should get paid an hour to do it, and then I price it at that." She felt the need to clarify one place that the vocational crept in, though: "I don't price it for the material used, I mean, because it is more for my pleasure and leisure so, that part I don't add to it." Her "pleasure and leisure," then, amounted to a discounted price for her artwork. Abbie, too, pointed to personal reasons for her low prices: "I have decided that I am way more interested in working than I am in that kind of career stuff. So I am fine with selling pieces at a price that people can afford to buy as long as it covers my materials. And, you know, *kind of* covers my time." Later, she explained why she didn't want to raise her prices to really cover her time: "I would rather sell work or place work in places that I think that . . . where it would be *good*, rather than to, you know, care about how much money I'm making." When we spoke, she had just sold four pieces to a very well-known specialist hospital, "which is a gorgeous building, gorgeous art everywhere. And that's important for me, to have my work in that kind of situation, because that kind of healing is a part of what I am going for. That's what I am trying to bring out in my work."

Armando, Land, and Abbie show how vocational accounts can be used to pull prices downward. But I saw artists use vocational accounts to inflate prices as well, as when Land told me about a few works she particularly liked: "I put stupid prices on, because I didn't want them to go away. I was like, I don't want to sell them. So I would put like really high prices, like thousands." Rudy told me the same thing, after telling me his favorite paintings were always the ones he was currently working on: "I'll put a high price on a painting just because I don't want to separate with it. Like that painting

right there, right now"—he pointed to one he had just completed—"I'd probably put a high price on it, but a year from now it'll be about half of that."

The relationships that form in practice between multiple orders of
worth are crucial to mapping the art community's contemporary landscape
of meaning. Marriages between accounts represent important, stable, and
widespread routes to value and legitimacy in this landscape. The ways that
artists deploy pecuniary and vocational accounts in concert can be used
instrumentally—to make an apparently sky-high price look reasonable, or
to explain why the low prices that mean an artist can't begin to cover her
costs are perfectly acceptable. As Elaine's story showed at the beginning of
this chapter, vocational accounts can alter the calculations demanded by
pecuniary logics, and the opposite is true as well: pecuniary accounts can
legitimate a vocationally driven narrative, bringing a practice otherwise
discussed in terms of leisure and pleasure into conversation with a profes-
sionalized, serious, full-time world of contemporary art practice. When we
begin with the literature rather than beginning with those we hope to understand, we can reify logical "conflicts" between meanings, whereas such
conflicts are part of—constitutive of—everyday lived experience. A house,
it is clear, is simultaneously a shelter and a home; we use it to build wealth
and memories both.[5]

. . .

Many times in my interviews with artists, they told me how important it
was to continue the work, how much they had sacrificed in order to practice
their art, how much more they were prepared to sacrifice. During one interview, late in the process of collecting data for this book, I sat at Alan's small
kitchen table, drank cold coffee, and asked about his partner, a woman he
had been with for many years. He told me about all the downsides of being
with another artist before he told me why none of it mattered: "I'm noticing
that it really helps. To kind of keep going with stuff. Even though you could
totally just stop." I had heard this refrain so many times—the acknowledg-
ment that you could, totally, just stop—that I mentioned how often artists
brought up attrition, how widespread the understanding was that, in fact,
quitting was always an option. An image came to my mind: artists' attempts
to keep working despite obstacles looks, depending on your squint, both

noble and ludicrous: like the people of the Netherlands, who have always fought the sea, will always fight the sea with an expensive, inconvenient, and occasionally failing system of dikes and sluices and spillways. Everyone knows very well that they could leave—that there are plenty of objectively lovely places in the world that sit well above sea level. But for the Dutch, there is special value to living in the Netherlands, and perhaps there's even a bit of disdain for the world without. Obviously, it is a social and a cultural process—not a genetic trait or purely instrumental logic—that allows such valuation to make sense, that allows the Dutch to continue fighting and living with the sea, this despite costs and effort and, sometimes, tragic deaths. I suggested the metaphor to Alan, telling him about the image in my head of the Netherlands and the sea a constant threat one must actively keep at bay. And he thought about whether the image was appropriate for a while. "I think so. Yeah." He paused for a moment. "I wonder if I could just stop, you know. But I don't. I don't stop."

Artists make economic offerings to the Muses, of course, but there are other sacrifices to be made as well. Artists told me stories of losses of confidence, of failed relationships and dysfunctional friendships, of incredible self-doubt, of inefficacy and illusory successes. Mark, originally trained as an architectural engineer, knew well how easy it would have been to quit working as an artist. He told me that keeping on required sacrifice: "I could go get a job, make a lot more money, and work a lot less hours if I wanted to. This is labor intensive work, and it's hard. It'd be a lot easier for me to go get a job with an engineering firm and be a project manager, make eighty or ninety thousand dollars a year, go to work forty hours a week and have a 401K and health insurance and benefits and all that." Then, after we'd been talking for several hours, he illustrated that sacrifice by admitting what it really looked like: "I've got a messed up shoulder that, after my next show, I'm going to have surgery on it. Being self-employed, if I can't use my shoulder, I don't work. Where, if I was working for a company, I'd have disability, or time off, or whatever. If I can't work, I don't make money." He awkwardly moved his arm a bit to show me his range of motion, and continued: "I have a detached bicep. It connects to the bone at the shoulder, and it's detached. I can't lift anything, I can't throw pots." He turned toward me, and pointed as he spoke: "They have to go in, they put two screws into your bone. Your bicep has this kind of cartilage ligament material at the end of the muscle that connects to the bone. They stitch that and tie the stitches around the screws and try to get it to grow back to the bone." He went back to the pot he was trimming. "This is my busy season, so I can't do it till December at the earliest. So I drink a lot." I probably looked a bit concerned when I asked—was he really putting surgery off for the next five months? He nodded grimly: "Or I don't eat in January." But quitting, finding work as a project manager and throwing pots on the weekends, wasn't ever a real option.

Among those artists who had seriously considered quitting—and among those former artists I met during my fieldwork who had, in fact, quit—it was always a combination of many factors and never simply a lack of financial resources that led to the impulse to "quit." But quitting, for the artists and self-defined ex-artists I spoke with, only rarely meant actually stopping painting, drawing, making sculpture; more often it meant going off the rails, becoming "just" an art teacher, "just" a portrait painter. When artists said someone had "quit" in this context, they referred to a departure from the communally defined "serious" pursuit of art, a move from one particular landscape of meaning into another. Derrek told me about someone who went too far down one path; looking for an appropriate analogy, he told me that when he said a friend had "quit," he didn't mean the guy never painted anymore. "Like a basketball player throwing paper balls in the trash can. It's not a basketball career." Then he laughed, a little uncomfortably. Each of the caricatures that defines the outer limits of the art world illuminates an exit route—and an invisible boundary worth avoiding, for fear you might accidentally step across.

.   .   .

Much of the literature on logics of action and value that take a structural or institutional view implies that such logics are stable and drive similar expressions and outcomes no matter the context.[6] A good deal of contemporary economic sociology, in contrast, is focused on showing when, why, and how even markets (arguably the most stable, important, and unbending of such logics) work differently, and mean different things, in different places and times.[7] The relationships between accounts discussed here—the dance between love and money, a landscape bound by caricature-sentries—are not "compromises," in which juxtapositions of diverse orders of worth are both temporary and fragile,[8] nor are they "ambiguities," in which flexible opportunists argue that first one, then another base of value is the one that counts.[9] The pairings and other relationships outlined here are constitutive of a field of practice and, as such, are remarkably stable. Individuals use multiple accounts in patterned ways to do specific things.

Diverse frameworks are not applied willy-nilly; the appropriate metaphor is neither the music sampler nor the toolbox. Rather, it might be useful to imagine these individuals as fashion designers looking for a new colorway. For the most part, these designers have a set palette of colors at their disposal, though occasionally the availability of new technologies, new collaborations outside the field, or the force of a particularly creative designer can make new colors possible.[10] Color theory helps us to "know" what colors match one another and to argue for the validity of such combinations—it can help us to understand "why" some colors look good together and others don't. The accounts and the marriages between accounts discussed above can be thought of as the combinations developed by these designers working through and then promoting a new colorway. For the most part, there are colors that we wear together, and colors that clash. But sometimes a new colorway just clicks: perhaps it fits the zeitgeist, or a celebrity is said to look good in it. Turquoise and purple don't go together—but then Lady Gaga shows up at Barney's selling a limited edition set of rings in those colors, and we collectively scratch our chins and say, well, maybe it does kind of work. When someone innovates, most often the new colorway, after some dissemination, fades into disuse, but on occasion it can lead to lasting change. While distinct orders of worth might be logically incompatible, accords between them are not empirically untenable, and in fact, some fields may be constructed so as to virtually require pairings and other groupings of diverse orders; compromises are likely inherent to the system.

In the previous chapter, I sketched a model of social processes of disagreement about value in working life. As an extant, valued field of activity—a tradition—is rationalized and becomes understood as properly an occupation—a job—tensions between distinct orders of worth become salient for some practitioners and come to be expressed in conflicts over the valuation of practice. Conflicts over the socially dominant valuation of practice take the form of diverse accounts of value and its bases by practitioners. In a context where occupational rationality and economic logic dominates, practitioners point to the limits of jobs when they insist on the inclusion of other bases of value. These conflicts take the form of distinct routes to valuation; they do not pit value against values, but aim to include some bases of value while excluding others. Some bases of value and routes to valuation achieve widespread resonance and become widely shared meanings within the community of practice, while others fall away. The degree to which an account draws on and fits within contemporary visions of traditional practice predicts its level of recognition by others. This process is one in which conflict over appropriate orders of worth is expressed in diverse and divergent valuations—a patterned, social process of disagreement about value and valuation.

We should expect to see these processes of "decommensuration" in working life in any field where a rationalized understanding of activity as valuable—as an occupation, a profession—overlaps well enough with traditional practice to largely supplant it, while fitting poorly enough to allow for conflict between traditional and occupational bases of value. Stated differently, we would expect to see conflicts over value in those fields of human activity that we engaged in before economic life in capitalism made some of them into "jobs": the care of young children, political work, religious work, and sports are just a few examples. These conflicts can seem strange, nonsensical, or inappropriate only because so much of what we do now is native to advanced capitalism, was developed in a world of near-total commensurability. But not everything is yet commensurable, and it's the rifts—the cracks that appear around the timeless human tasks of preparing food for one another, talking politics, raising children, pursuing love and sex, friendship, creative production, and community—that continue to raise hell as we move closer to entirely commensurable lives. While the content of each step of the process outlined here—the divergent valuations, the historical imaginaries—would surely differ in other fields, the process would look much the same. And as in the visual arts, recurring relationships between multiple orders of worth would be constitutive of the field's landscape of practice.

Today, the dance between love and money is central to legitimacy in the art world, and in that world, four types of account come together to enable a historically, culturally, and locally specific vision of the artist and the value of the artist's work. If we wear it often enough and around the right people, turquoise no longer clashes with purple. Those who continue to argue you can't wear them together look terribly old-fashioned, cut off from the real world of experimentation, action, and cultural change. But they are still out there, whether they're color-blind or simply refusing to accept the new rules. And when they have power, they can wreak havoc on complex and evolving fields like the visual arts.

Doing Things with Words

6

ANN IS A SCULPTOR, PAINTER, AND FILMMAKER; she also works as a scenic artist. When we met in a sunny ice cream parlor, she pulled out her computer, and moving quickly through images from dozens of films, she pointed out things she had done: she showed me brickwork she had made from scratch to fit a film's era, fake walls she'd built. "I had to *make* that old-fashioned linoleum. I actually had to make that, tile by tile." It is clear to me, rereading the transcript from our conversation, that she knows she is speaking to someone who knows little about her profession. "There's one real wall and then two fake walls. The fake walls have to look like the real wall. So the wood grain has to match and the marble has to match." She showed me a photo of an old house with a fence, and told me about making them: "In this scene, a train goes through a fence. We had to make the fence look like it had been there for fifty years, so we had to make all the wood look really old. And when the train goes through, we had to have the pieces of wood fly up in the air and look like they were really old pieces of wood. Even though they were all brand-new." She was speaking both to and about me when she said, later, "A lot of people just don't really get that there's scenic art that's done for movies." When I asked what she thought people saw of her work in a finished movie, she said simply, "They don't see. I would say 90% of the people do not see. They don't have . . . they're shocked when they discover they're not seeing what they think they're seeing." For much of our conversation, I was one of these 90%, and she tried to educate me—but suddenly, near the end of our interview, she included me in her circle, in the other 10%. We were talking about films, and found that we both enjoyed a particular type of staginess. The film *Moonrise Kingdom* had recently opened, and in talking about it, we moved into a shared space.

I had asked whether she had seen anything recently that she loved. She exclaimed, eyes shining: "Oh my God. *Moonrise Kingdom*." I nodded, leaned in: "Oh, yeah. That was a beautiful movie." She began to tell me, with a knowing tone, precisely why I thought so: "Now, that is a really cool movie for a couple of reasons, because that movie has elements that are obviously fantasy, but they're so perfectly done that it works. Like all those hokey little tents that are so corny but very wonderful. It's like a fairy tale come to life." I broke in, maybe cut her off a bit: "Yeah. All of his visual worlds are really immersive when you're actually watching them. And I find it strange to watch them because I think you're very aware . . ." Ann jumped in again: "But it's a fairy tale. It's like all . . ." And I cut her off in turn: "It's rare that you're successfully that drawn into something that you're also hyperaware of as unreal." She beamed. "Right! I mean every aspect. The costume, the little girl and her blue eye shadow and short dresses and the cool yellow suitcase. I mean, every aspect of it is really hyperintensified. It's a stereotype. It's a cartoon, almost, like a living and breathing cartoon."

Ann made a subtle shift during this exchange. Until that point—for most of our interview, in fact—she had spoken to me as a curious outsider, walking me step by step through the intricacies of her work. In this passage, she started by telling me why the movie was a good one; she thought, perhaps, that I liked it but didn't have a well-developed critique. She said, "Now, that is a really cool movie for a couple of reasons . . ." and began to tell me those reasons. I responded by indicating that I, too, had thought, for the same reasons, that the film was "cool." She first broke into my point, still teaching me something, but then, satisfied that I had something to say that might be relevant to the conversation ("Right!"), built on it instead. After this, the tone of our interview changed, and she treated me as someone who was, at least as regards fine art, on the same page. She made a point through a quick reference to *The Gift*, a book that was at the time of the interview recirculating in a particular kind of high-art circle on the West Coast, and was satisfied that I caught her meaning.[1] These objects—a movie, a book—served as a sort of shorthand, allowing us to figure out where we stood vis-à-vis one another.

.   .   .

Conflicts about value—Do we do this for love, or for money? Is this a job or a calling? Do I deserve payment, or is an audience in itself my reward?—play out in a coherent social process of disagreement, where logics that fit occupational practice collide with rationales pulled from our memories of traditional practice. From this mix, new meanings emerge, new ways of being. They can appear at first illogical, even incoherent, but in their uses they are stable, allowing practitioners to make sense of themselves and to demand recognition.

Why are these new meanings sometimes so hard to see, especially for outsiders? Why do so many insist on a never-waning dualism between love and money, when all evidence points to the centrality of their generative alliance? Recall that I expected at first to find logical coherence in artists' narratives and distinct, separate "types" attached to these narratives, one per story: the bits of paper sliding around my desk, my failure of parsimony. I hoped to find a formula for the proper placement of sidewalks, one that would work in any landscape, but every time I laid a grid, I saw that the people populating the world I was interested in ignored it entirely, sticking instead to footpaths they'd made themselves. I decided, rather than fencing off the grassy areas, to follow those tracks through the landscape. I have tried to map the footpaths and to see whether some were more well-traveled than others, their lanes cut more deeply.

Looking back, I expected more distinct and disparate orders of worth to emerge, thanks not only to some presumption of logical coherence generally but also, more specifically, to my everyday understanding of the rules of public argument, in which to win one must not admit to nuance.[2] I have shown instead how multiple orders of worth are engaged by actors simultaneously, without issue. I suggest, in fact, that such relationships between multiple orders of worth may be constitutive of a field's landscape of practice. Accords between distinct orders of worth are not empirically untenable, and some fields—especially fields in which quality and value are front and center, as in fields that are undergoing processes of transition from tradition to occupation—may allow or even require alliances between diverse orders to structure meaning. But why have I seen so much of this conflict and complexity, when public life requires such certainty?

In public, we assume a context-specific requirement of logical coherence, and we adopt a limited array of tactics to minimize diverse or potentially discrepant accounts, in keeping with the demands of the context. The conflicts, arguments, negotiations, and meanings of interest to this study take place largely in interaction; they can be invisible to the analyst of secondary sources, who may encounter them only once the revaluations inherent to these processes are brought to the public in coherent form by elites and social movements. The contexts of my research—the interactive and communicative moments that make up the bulk of the data under consideration here—were crucial to my ability to access and apprehend the processes at the heart of this study.

The space between each of my respondents and me was filled with shared meanings; in an interview (especially one embedded in a process of participant observation, as many of mine were), a respondent has an enormous range of meaningful semantic and narrative objects from which to draw. This range of possibilities makes apparently illogical, complex, nuanced, and ambiguous accounts more likely to be deployed than in a public setting. Between you and me, there is an *us* that (however temporary) allows for an ease of movement, a comfortable conversation, and plenty of agency and creativity in our uses of language.[3]

Anyone who has spoken in front of a group knows how different such an experience is from one-on-one or small-group interactions. Speaking in front of a potentially diverse group of strangers, is another step removed from the intimacy and negotiation of a one-on-one conversation; speaking in public, to a more certainly diverse and potentially hostile audience, is again a step removed. When I speak at a university, for example, I try to be careful both to limit my accounts to those that are presumably legible in such a setting, in which I am able to assume many shared experiences, and to simultaneously "check my privilege" by interrogating my assumptions about those shared experiences. The space between myself and a classroom—the shared space we create, for a while—is more narrow than it would be between me and any one student in the room in one-on-one conversation, and allows for significantly less movement.

Speaking in public, especially when it is known that such speech will be recorded and available forevermore, narrows the range of possibility even more. Writing, especially in today's searchable landscape, yet more. Writing for a niche magazine might be just a bit more constrained than speaking in front of a classroom; if I write for an art magazine based in the western United States and read by well-educated contemporary artists, I can use a good deal of shorthand, perhaps be a bit creative in my use of language without too much fear of terrible misreadings of my work. But if I write for a general readership outlet with a national reach, especially if I am hoping not to be seen as inappropriately biased, I have far less leeway. Crucially, in these last paragraphs I have been speaking only of the wish to be understood—to not draw too heavily on secret knowledges, to "make sense" to as many others as possible. Making sense is only the first step in much public writing; many are also hoping to be convincing, to win an argument, to gain something. To convince others in public usually requires some adherence to the rules of public argument, and those rules promote logically coherent argumentation. It is no surprise that, in looking to such texts, analysts so often find a sort of logical coherence.

An early inkling of the importance of context came for me when I compared the public writings of a few of the artists I had spoken with to the transcripts of my conversations with them. Aside from the differences we expect generally from comparisons of written and spoken language, one distinction struck me—when these artists spoke in public, even for art audiences, they were consistently less nuanced, more straightforward, and much more coherent than they were in conversation with me. This was true whether the secondary sources I was able to find were published texts authored by the artists, interviews presumably edited by someone else, or videotaped discussions or presentations. The distinction was not one between spoken and written language; it was, rather, a difference between interactive and public contexts. I have laid out a model of conflict about value in working life with three stages, and communicative contexts are crucial to all three.

I was generally seen by the artists I spoke with as relatively knowledgeable about art, thanks in part to my then still-googlable background working as an artist. Before I began graduate work in sociology, I worked as an artist, and that experience did leave me with a wealth of tacit knowledge. I am, for a sociologist, a relative insider, though primarily to one subculture among a vast constellation of overlapping but distinct art worlds, and with a dated membership card. I was addressed as a sort-of insider by the majority of those that I interviewed. The specifics of my past weren't always clear to the artists I spoke with, as when Bodie, after our formal interview, asked what kind of work I had done; I told him, and after a few moments, he said, a little embarrassed, "Oh, I could have not needed to say lots of that. You know, you have to explain so much when people don't know project work." My position vis-à-vis most of the artists I spoke with—vaguely knowledgeable but clearly no longer practicing, more "inside" than most outsiders but definitely not a full member of the community—was, I think, a useful one, allowing me to ask "dumb" questions in order to hear the ways that individuals would articulate their answers, while also permitting a measure of inside baseball.

When respondents pointed directly to my background as an indication that we two—we two here, now, in conversation, 'get it,' share a meaning, they showed how interaction is so often at the core of meaning-making. They also suggested reasons that the conflicts over value of interest here look quite different in public, when they appear at all. The accounts under consideration in this study are highly situated in the interview setting, in a particular kind of communicative act, and in interaction with me as a somewhat knowledgeable interlocutor. The artists I spoke with drew from a landscape of meanings that they believed that we two shared, because they aimed in our interaction to have their actions and accounts make sense to me.[4]

In interactive contexts speakers are able to draw on a wide array of meanings, thanks to their understanding of shared context, histories, and experiences; furthermore, in interactive contexts, speakers can gauge listeners' understanding, and modify their speech as necessary. In my research, I cannot know in any depth how I was seen by the artists I met, but in conversation, they drew on their perceptions of my background, experience, and understandings regularly, as when they said, "You're an artist, so . . ." or "you've got kids; you know." Think back to my conversation with Ann, with her changing perception of me midway through.

Throughout that conversation, Ann and I populated our interindividual territory with both experiential and textual anchors, and slowly made sense of one another.[5] Later in our discussion, when we had been talking about her own work, I asked whether she felt she was often able to create something clearly constructed as a part of her job, something like the stagy films we both like. I asked about one particular film she had told me she had worked on, one that I thought of as very stylized and constructed, with the visuals a crucial element of the movie's content. Recall that she had earlier insisted that "90% of the people do not see" her work. Now that she included me in the other 10%, she pointed directly at my past when she dismissed the notion that anyone else would have noticed her work: "I feel like that's pretty stylized. Still *you* only know because . . . regular people don't know that." I protested that I was fairly "regular," and she shot me down: "OK, but you're an artist."

The artists I spoke with were very aware of the need for a straightforward and coherent public face as an artist—this was most apparent when some agonized about the ways that their "names" were out there, working against them. The problems they pointed to as part of their public image were rarely things that they minimized, downplayed, or avoided in their talks with me; in conversation, these were part of a rich past, not a contradictory present.

Sophie tried not to worry that the screen-printed works she had once been proud of were visibly for sale through a Google search of her name, but knew that, for many, the first impression that she was an illustrator who made posters might sully her attempt to position herself as a fine art sculptor. During her conversation with me, she told me quite proudly about the prints as part of her back story, and constructed a narrative in which their production supported her trajectory as an artist. But she still worried, because in public, things have to be simple; they have to make sense immediately, and she chafed at the internet-enabled dismissal of her work as "commercial" that may well happen. Gregory talked at length about his name being corrupted by his past and current employment when I asked how he introduced himself to others: "This has actually been the big question this year. It is really upsetting and challenging. A lot of the same institutions that I would want to take notice of me as an artist, now or later on, are starting to look at this project that I did, and that I began with this company, and be like, oh, we would kind of want something like that for us." The problem was, the institutions that he hoped for attention from were the very types most likely to know about, and find uses for, the work he did in his day job. "Fancy nonprofits who support artists are thinking, 'You know what? We need someone like that to make like a cool artist's multiple tote bag or something that we can have as a giveaway at our gala.' Or, 'We would like to have like an artist's multiple that isn't a book,' you know what I mean, 'as part of this show.'" Being seen the wrong way—as someone who could provide that tote bag—was awful: "Of course it's terrifying because you're like, wait a minute, that's not what I set out to do, this was, like, something I *could* do, you know, but my relationship to identity becomes really complicated, because my name basically could mean a lot of things, and I'm trying *so hard* to preserve it as the name of an artist." When we spoke, Gregory was turning thirty-two, and felt lost: "Almost every creative identity I've had is somehow parceled out, either as a collaboration or my association with this company. So something that's really typical for so many artists, to just be their own name, be like, I am Joe Smith, I'm a sculptor, and I've been that way since I was twenty, it's just not true for me."

Gregory hid nothing about his employment in our conversation together. Like Sophie, in conversation with me, Gregory wove the story of his employment into a narrative trajectory that supported his identification as an independent artist. But he was nervous about how it looked in public, worried about what people would think if they weren't able to see his paid work as part of a creative practice that was focused elsewhere—able to see it as he saw it, and as he hoped that I saw it. Gregory was concerned about the accounts that were out there, floating around, reaching people before he could sit them down and make them understand. Both Gregory and Sophie had faith in their ability to feel out a shared landscape of meaning and cast their pasts in terms that made sense, that supported their preferred account with an in-time interlocutor, as they had with me—what they were worried about was the first impression, the public stance that a first Google hit can today define.

In public, we all *know* that we are expected to be coherent, consistent; further, we know that if we only get time to make one point, we have to make it as clearly and explicitly as possible. Gregory and Sophie were worried that the single point that would come across was the wrong one—an issue that is minimized in one-on-one and interactive contexts. In interaction, individuals can reconfigure meanings, place them in time and space, compare and contrast and marry them to other meanings in agentic ways. It's only in public, where we're frozen in amber for all to see, that we need to be careful to cohere.

There are rules to public speech. Anyone who has learned to write op-eds knows: to get published, hit one point, and hit it hard. Two issues might cloud research based on public speech and secondary sources in general; the first, that of a limited and skewed sample of the population, is simple. Even if you follow the rules, you might not get published; most don't, so authors need to flash whatever shiny baubles they've got—an executive title, a fancy degree. In their focus on those who speak in such contexts (elites, broadly speaking), analysts often minimize the differences between those who speak in public and the population at large. We know, to use the example of the op-ed page, that these writers are heavily skewed male, elite, and white in the U.S. context.[6] It is of course plausible for some questions to assume, when we look to the kinds of public writing that secondary sources are often drawn from, that we are speaking of "dominant" cultures, and that "dominant" usefully overlaps with the populations relevant to the sources used, but this specification minimizes the reach of our theorization about the ways that diverse orders of worth function in everyday life.

We are more likely to see complex accounts in interaction primarily because speakers are able to draw on a wide variety of meanings as part of a broad shared landscape. This second issue should by now be obvious. No matter how different we may be, we look for shared experience when we hope to make a difficult point. And in one-on-one interactions, a speaker can always gauge their interlocutor's understanding, can restate and rephrase until they are confident that they have gotten their meaning across. I cannot overstate how many times this happened during my interviews. Respondents made assumptions about my background that allowed them to gloss over an important element of their story; they picked up on a slight furrow in my brow and circled back to the issue, clarifying it. Artists who were unsure about the extent to which we shared a background often dropped names and cited specific artworks, artists, experiences—all of them shorthand for a bit of landscape, a set of meanings they might be able to draw on to build an account I would understand. Interactive one-on-one and small-group communicative contexts allow for the complex and ambiguous narratives that are of interest here as instances of conflict, negotiation, and revaluation. By looking as researchers to more diverse sources of data we might refine a theory of diverse orders of worth in working life that accounts for more (and more diverse) cases. We gain enormously from taking the generative power of complexity seriously.

Particular communicative contexts limit and promote different ways of doing things with words. In conversation with others, we can take risks; we can be confusing. We can speak in subtle, ambiguous, even incoherent ways, knowing that the plot will resolve by the end, that on the whole we can make sense—we can even make new sense. The things we do with words in conversation might reach fewer people, but we can do more things with the words we have. We can do things with words, together.

.   .   .

I take as a given that economic and market logics dominate in public life and especially in working life—that "everything has its price," and that, as the idiom suggests, we all know it. Thus, I presuppose a socially dominant route to the valuation of practice. In an increasingly occupationalized art field, the expanding power of market logic is central to the shift from traditional practice to occupational rationality. The transformation of a tradition to a job involves many aspects—organized training and credentialing, increased bureaucratization and fit with state and institutional structures, the development of professional identities—all of which are deeply influenced by and understood in terms of a market order of worth.[7] But as I have shown, our memories of not-yet-dead traditions allow for and shape spaces of conflict, where both old modes of valuation and new accounts of value can resonate and can become widely accepted meanings.

The norm of work as paid employment has real effects on the development of identity and practice, both for individuals with stable employment and those without.[8] Even those entirely outside the everyday world of work must often successfully classify themselves as workers in order to access welfare, political, or field-specific benefits.[9] Much of the scholarship on the

centrality of working life has addressed individual occupations; these studies have shown that work identities seem necessary even, or perhaps especially, for those who are without jobs.[10] The richest point of overlap between
the literature on working life and research on value and valuation has been
in studies of care work and gendered labor. Researchers looking at what
has traditionally been women's work, carried out as part of a household
economy and without pay, have shown how unrecognized labor influences
well-being,[11] have asked how gender strategies influence household economies,[12] and have investigated when and how labor is legitimized as work.[13]
Most relevant to the present study, many have shown how women engaged
in care work generally acknowledge the dominance of economic thinking
before calling instead on alternative metrics of value.[14] Literature on "invisible work" tends to draw on the gendered work tradition and carries it to
less gendered arenas,[15] but there remains a wealth of rich possibilities for
investigation of this juncture.

This is a book about visual artists. Many think that artists are unique,
special, different from the rest of us. But visual artists are a useful window
on value and on processes of valuation, especially at this historical moment.
There was a time, not long ago, when many Americans shared one goal: they
aimed to work for one company for forty years, then retire. And there was
a system that worked, for the lucky and privileged at least, with pensions
and insurance and a gold watch at the end. Writing these words, though, I
know how illusory that goal was even then, how few were able to share in
its pleasures. And I know even better how distant that vision of working life
is from what my peers experience. Today, those of us lucky enough to find
good work switch jobs—even careers—at the drop of a hat, the whim of an
employer.[16]

In the past decade, I have been employed, self-employed, and unemployed. I have been paid for my time by the hour, by the piece, and by the
year. I have given a good deal of work away for free. For a little over a year, I
received paid parental leave, and two years later, I received a year's salary as
an award. As I wrote the first draft of this book, I sat between stools; I was a
graduate student, an apprentice to masters, in a complicated economic uni-
verse. I was paid by the hour for administrative work I did for my department but when I taught I was paid an honorarium completely untethered

to the actual hours that I worked, the efforts I could document, or student outcomes. I carried out research that may or may not ensure some sort of career, for which I was most often unpaid. Occasionally, I was able to secure awards from my department or university that reimbursed small portions of the material costs of my research, because I did it not only on my own behalf but also in their name. I was a member of an unrecognized union, one that would have been legitimate had I been a student at a public university but, since I matriculated at a private institution, one that remained more or less meaningless. Today, I sit editing the final manuscript; for the last two years I have been employed by a university in Sweden, and as such I work for the state. I receive a monthly salary, but only my teaching hours—20% of my position—are policed, and those very loosely: the way those hours are calculated was negotiated by others and is, again, entirely untethered to either the hours I work or the outcomes of that labor. What is my time worth? My skills? These years? What yardstick should I use to measure that worth—the dollar, or something else, something more?

Although stable, paid employment serves as the basis for most of our ideas about work, a great many of us do not fit that mold. Self-employment, as a category, bursts at the seams with diverse and divergent practices. Temporary, contingent, contract, and freelance workers often lack a clear employer, a stable workplace, or a single occupation. While issues of work, quality, and value are especially apparent in the visual arts, they are of course not specific to that field. With artists' stories, we can learn about the ways that the nontraditionally employed define the value of their work, and perhaps we can understand something about the effects of changing, contingent, and contentious valuation.

Valuation drives the choices we make and shapes our claims. When we can't make the world understand—when our accounts of value aren't legible to others, or when we are confronted by rules written for another time, a different landscape of value—the consequences can be serious.

The Audit of Venus

7

THE FIRST TIME I SPOKE WITH VENUS DEMARS, an artist and musician from Minnesota, she called after midnight from her sister's backyard up on the North Shore in the summer of 2013. I wanted to talk to her about an audit she was going through with the state tax authorities; I had heard it was something more than a simple mismatch between receipts. She called me late, after playing a concert, and told me her story—out of breath, pacing in the dark. At the end of our conversation, I posed a silly question, though I already knew the answer: Isn't the worst-case scenario here just a change in tax status, maybe a little bit of money to pay back? What does it matter?

Her voice caught. "It feels like it's discrediting me as a person," she said, "and just throwing my twenty-year career out the window. Saying, 'you were just playing the whole time.' You put your heart and soul out on the line because that's what touches people. And then they tell you that everything you're doing is just pretend. It can crush you."

What happens when art becomes work? Artmaking today is a job, an occupation, a profession for ever-increasing numbers—but it is a strange one, in that it doesn't always come with a paycheck. We live in a world of "What do you do?" at first meetings, of occupation as identity.[1] The idea of the "working artist" is not defined by training, employers, income, or the other usual markers of an occupation. It's interpreted variously but always emphatically, a pose necessary for participation in most art worlds today. But turning art into work pulls issues of quality and value front and center; it props open a door and invites conflict about value. How that conflict plays out—what we think, how we think it, and whose ideas win out—sculpts our work. It shapes the things that we do, what we feel is right to do, appropriate, legitimate. It shapes the objects we make, which ones are shown, what is highly valued. It shapes how we ask to be paid, and whether we are.

Our beliefs about value—the stories we tell ourselves, and one another—have real, concrete ramifications. Beliefs are enshrined in law and other institutions; in turn, they structure the accounts people are willing and able to give. I look here at a tax audit: a rare site of conflict between artists and the state in the United States. Such audits are a crystallization of the conflicts discussed in this book between diverse forms of value, and Venus's story shows how deeply these debates can cut. Art has turned into work, but the transformation hasn't been easy, and it isn't complete.

When we first spoke, Venus had been the subject of an audit by the Minnesota Department of Revenue for about a year. Venus is an artist and, since she makes money from her artwork, she's a small businessperson. She didn't hold a day job and had made about $30,000 from her artwork that year: selling drawings and concert tickets, sometimes receiving grants for her performance work. For more than a decade she had worked with an accountant to file a Schedule C each year, an itemization of profits and losses that small businesspeople in the United States file along with their personal income taxes. With that Schedule C, she and twenty-three million other self-employed workers are able to write off business expenses, everything from tubes of paint to record sleeves. For many, those deductions make doing business possible. But in 2013, the Minnesota Department of Revenue issued an opinion ruling Venus to be, officially, a hobbyist.

We could understand something about Venus's experience by thinking about the classification of artists: who counts, and who doesn't. How to define the population of artists, and to what end, is a lively methodological debate among cultural policy and arts researchers.[2] Sociological perspectives try to deal with the complexities of occupational commitments to the arts and the particularities of careers in the knowledge, experience, and culture industries. These perspectives range from those that acknowledge a performance of commitment to be an indicator of professional status among artists[3] to those that would simply sweep the great mass of artists into a bucket labeled amateurs and volunteers.[4]

We could understand something else about Venus and her ordeal by thinking in terms of rules. Weber defined bureaucracy in large part around rule-following, and acknowledged that it could seem unhuman, even dehumanizing. But he argued that at its best, rule-following could minimize bias and favoritism and promote equality.[5] He wrote, "The more the bureaucracy is 'dehumanized,' the more completely it succeeds in eliminating from official business love, hatred, and all purely personal, irrational, and emotional elements which escape calculation. This is the specific nature of bureaucracy and it is appraised as its special virtue."[6] More recent work from social psychologists would add cognitive bias to the love and hate that we would prefer to avoid in our dealings with tax authorities.[7] Rules can feel restrictive, and many chafe at the slow rate of change in bureaucracies. But in general, in our dealings with the state, we do prefer clear, transparent rules. As Charles Perrow wrote in his defense of rule-following, "people make rules, and people are not generally geniuses. The problem is not rules in general, but particular ones that need changing."[8]

But the audit of Venus is about more than all that. It's about artmaking, and identity, and about how the two tie into an auditor's ability to differentiate between installation art and construction work. It's about the complexities of occupational commitments to the arts, and about the particularities of careers in the culture industries, and about a less-than-traditional marriage between high school sweethearts. It's about a place with a diverse and complex cultural life, thanks in part to our collective disinterest in policing whether or not anyone is a "real" artist. And it's both about and not about Venus, unclassifiable but not ambivalent, who tries to think the best of everyone.

Finally, this is a story about value. It's about the discrepant stories artists have to tell when they argue on behalf of their work: on the one hand, it's a calling; on the other, their choices are calculated and careerist. It's about how we listen to those stories, and how hard it can be to hold both in our heads at once. It's about understanding the dance between love and money, and about what it means when we can't, or won't.

.   .   .

When I went to visit her, Venus invited me to the home in south Minneapolis that she bought in 1986 with her wife, Lynette Reini-Grandell, a poet and college professor. Inside, a bright porch opened to a richly colored home. Out back, a carriage house sheltered enormous in-progress paintings and a tour van. The Venus I met that day was a soft-spoken woman, screened by lush greenery on her front porch, sitting amid a pile of receipts, and creating a detailed spreadsheet like nothing I'd ever seen. A few days later I said goodnight to another Venus, a slim fifty-three-year-old recovering from the heart surgery he had undergone two weeks earlier, wearily heading down to the basement to knock out half an hour's rehab on the treadmill, accompanied by his loving wife of more than thirty years on the exercise bike. Another night, Venus stood alone with a guitar and tight black jeans at the front of a low-ceilinged room, filled the space with her voice, and brought her audience to tears. Venus came out as trans twenty years ago, and has lived between genders since. She wore heavy eyeliner and her hair was dyed in a two-tone homage to Cruella de Vil, but these were the only direct nods to her outsize stage persona as the leader of the genderqueer glam punk band she had fronted for the past twenty years. That's not relevant to this story, except when it maybe is. We sat on her front porch that first day and snacked on nuts while we talked.

One might imagine that artists don't know—or care—much about the intricacies of tax law. They don't talk about art and taxes in mixed company. It's a little too instrumental. A bit gauche, really. Talking about the business side of things, what it really means to make a living in the arts, to commit to the arts as an occupation as well as a vocation, can look, to outsiders, like a denial of the sorts of dreamy pronouncements artists often make in public. But artists aren't distant from or disdainful of the realities of everyday life. As we have seen, doing it for love and doing it for money aren't irreconcilable in arts practice—but it turns out that the state continues to insist on and uphold that imaginary incompatibility, despite all evidence to the contrary.

Venus, like most artists, had done a range of jobs over the years. Design work at a t-shirt business, some landscaping. But she hadn't held a traditional day job since 1996. She's best known for her music, but is also a respected filmmaker and performance artist, and shows and sells paintings and drawings. She has been awarded the big grants that local artists aim for, and while I was in town I asked around about her. Everyone in the arts community knew who she was, and knew about the audit, and had a strongly held opinion. Many of them were terrified on their own behalf. If this can happen to Venus, what about me?

There are a few pieces of tax lore that are widely circulated by artists; among small businesspeople in other fields you can find such stories as well, each pointing to a different understanding of the costs and benefits of engagement with the state. Andy Warhol, in particular, is a touchstone in the arts—he went too far in a poster that depicted Richard Nixon in sickly green and drew his wrath, so the story goes, and was terrorized by annual audits until his early death. In response, he kept the *Diaries*, with entries for each two-dollar cab ride alongside gossip about the Jaggers and insights into his life and work, and swept all the detritus of his life into the *Time Capsules* to overwhelm the Internal Revenue Service with evidence of his practice, its daily rhythms, its costs.[9] This is the story that gets passed around, depicting a capricious state and an artist who rises to its challenge with lasting aesthetic statements.

There are no good data out there on the number of artists filing Schedule Cs or the proportion that are audited annually. Presumably, the tax authorities keep records, but they do not publish the numbers. According to the Census Bureau, one third of the two million artists in the United States are self-employed; they make up, then, a small proportion of the country's Schedule C filers, all of whom are at a relatively high risk of audit each year, according to several accountants I spoke with. Venus and her wife filed their taxes jointly, and they each filed a Schedule C: Venus as an artist, Lynette as a poet. They kept their receipts, and they followed the law. As well as anyone could.

When Venus and Lynette found out they were being audited by the State of Minnesota for the tax years 2009 through 2011, they thought they might have inadvertently missed a small payment or expense. Getting audited is a pain, but it's part of doing business. Venus initially compared it to being called in for jury duty. "We thought it was just, assemble your receipts, and make sure the math works . . ." said Lynette. She broke off, laughing. She took a breath, and told me that they found some receipts they'd missed when they did their taxes, and thought they might actually come out ahead and get a little refund. She laughed again, more bitterly this time, and shook her head: "That was incredibly naïve." She and Venus spent a few months gathering receipts and other paperwork in the evenings, signed over their power of attorney to their accountant, and sent him to a meeting with the auditor.

John Marg-Patton was the couple's accountant. He said that, after some explanation, the auditor seemed to understand how both Venus's and Lynette's businesses worked, and John expected to get a call within a few weeks, maybe to quibble over $200 here or there. Maybe there was a credit card receipt for gas where the name of the town couldn't be read. Nothing out of the ordinary.

The auditor called John and asked for another meeting. He wanted some clarification on each of the businesses. John asked Venus and Lynette to come in and explain what they did, so they packed up boxes stuffed with evidence of their long careers: magazine articles, reviews, publications, posters, and records. The four of them met in the Department of Revenue's offices. Venus still had these boxes when we met, and a quick scan of their contents suggests a well-documented independent career in the arts: reviews of her music in foreign-language publications, professionally designed posters from two decades of tours, hard copies of albums, invitations to exhibition openings, contracts.

The auditor didn't want to see any of it. The meeting didn't go as smoothly as they'd hoped. Venus tried to show the auditor articles about her, even some international coverage, but he wasn't interested. "I started showing him all of the magazines, and he looks and goes, 'I don't need that. I know, I know, big transgender rock star. I'm a suburban white guy, I'm over it. I'm a numbers guy, let's talk numbers.'"

John told me he was surprised that the auditor had, as he put it, "done quite a bit of lookup on the computer . . . no auditor that I know of ever talks about doing research on people they're auditing." The auditor told Lynette that he'd looked her up on ratemyprofessors.com. The site encourages students to rate professors on their looks as well as their teaching ("Is your professor hot? Hot professors get a red chili pepper."), and the tone of the ratings is often juvenile and can skew toward the disgruntled. Lynette was horrified, and the meeting was difficult for both Venus and Lynette. But they came out of it satisfied that the auditor now understood how their businesses worked, and they were confident that the numbers would shake out.

The auditor called and asked for another meeting; he said a couple of things still weren't clear, and he needed to understand the businesses better. Venus and Lynette came in for a second meeting. Lynette, whose primary income comes from her work as a professor (a position closely tied to her poetry practice), went through her records to find copies of all her rejection letters from literary journals. She had to show that she was trying to make money from her poetry—and that she was failing. Businesses don't always succeed right away. The point, it seems, is to try—to have a "profit motive," in the words of the Department of Revenue. So when you go into your meeting with your auditor, you might have to explain how many more times you've tried and failed, to recount the rejections that never made it to paper. "To demonstrate that I had been trying, and getting rejected, for a long period of time," as Lynette put it. I didn't stifle a shocked bark of a laugh, and she laughed too: "I know. We can laugh now, we can laugh now. Yeah. When you're in the middle of it, it just . . . well."

Artists are especially vulnerable to the ambiguous requirements of the tax authorities. The guidelines published by the IRS and used by the Minnesota Department of Revenue and other states' tax agencies dictate that "an activity qualifies as a business if your primary purpose for engaging in the activity is for income or profit." Motives and intentions are tough to prove. Artists have an especially hard time showing that the primary purpose of their activities is income, given that generations of artists have been taught to act as though they make art for love, not money. The truth— that love and money are deeply interconnected in occupational artistic practice—is something that artists can acknowledge in interaction, but it's too complicated for public consumption. A distance from filthy lucre, then, is a normal part of the pose of the professional artist. And that is how a bad rule becomes potentially devastating. An entire generation of economic sociologists writing after Zelizer have shown, again and again, that economic life need not pit value against values.[10] Love and money, so obviously intertwined for professional artists, are inexorably linked for the rest of us as well. But not everyone is yet on board.

The IRS circulates nine "factors" it considers when determining whether a given taxpayer should classify their activities as a hobby or a business. Tax attorneys and CPAs know they move in a vast grey area with ample room for prejudice when they try to navigate these guidelines: the factors include "whether you carry on the activity in a businesslike manner" and "whether the time and effort you put into the activity indicate you intend to make it profitable."

Venus and Lynette both received preliminary determinations from the state, reclassifying them as hobbyists rather than self-employed artists. That meant they could no longer file as self-employed or deduct expenses, and owed thousands of dollars in back taxes, penalties, and interest. In nine points, the state outlined its argument against each of them. Lynette had just won a large grant, a realistic source of income in Minnesota, with its highly developed nonprofit arts landscape, but the auditor stated she had not shown that "relying on grant income is a viable business strategy." The auditor criticized Venus for using the same credit card for personal and business expenses, and was not pleased that she didn't have a written business plan, insisting that "there was no documentation provided that indicated any formal business analysis was conducted." But the rest of the arguments against her didn't make much sense.

Venus had lugged a box of old tour posters to her meetings with the auditor—that box of materials he wouldn't look at, saying he was just a "numbers guy." The determination read, "There was no documentation provided that the taxpayer promoted his 'tours.'" The auditor argued that Venus should have been "renting performance space and selling tickets for the performance" herself, rather than performing in established clubs. Despite the newspaper and magazine reviews Venus had tried to show the auditor, he wrote: "There was no oral or written testimony provided to indicate the taxpayer had his music, or art, evaluated by talent professionals." The auditor decided that Venus's commissioned mural and mosaic work was not a part of her artistic practice but, rather, "freelance construction activity."

One section of Venus's determination read, "The presence of personal motives in carrying on of an activity may indicate that the activity is not engaged in for profit." Underneath, bullet points outlined evidence against her. In just a few words, the auditor's letter called into question a centuries-old understanding of art as an expression of the artist's soul. He recast an aesthetic choice (and savvy brand-building strategy) as a black mark on Venus's record, and relied on the myth of money as the antithesis of love to discredit her. The first point read simply: "The music and art are self-created by the taxpayer and based on his life experience and perspective, and are intensely personal." The exact same dismissal was cut-and-pasted into Lynette's determination: "The poetry created by the taxpayer is based on her life experience and perspective, and is intensely personal."

John received the determinations first, and read them over the telephone to Venus, who paced back and forth as she fumed. She asked John if they should get a lawyer. He paused, then said he thought they probably should. Later, recounting the moment, she told me: "When he said yes, then I just felt, 'oh my God, this is crazy.' I always trusted the government. I always trusted the machine to do what it should."

Venus told me a story about when she was a boy with a mohawk back in Duluth. She ran down the street because she was late, and was stopped by a police officer. He couldn't believe she wasn't up to no good, but she told him the truth—why she was running and where she was going—and he understood, and he let her go. She'd had a lifetime of run-ins with power, and in all of those instances, other people's individual discretion was at work. And she always told the truth, and everything always worked out. This time, she was involved in a conflict that shouldn't have been about her personal qualities, but about marks on paper, about the numbers. And she didn't know how to think about the fact that the machine seemed to be failing her.

Venus and Lynette began to raise money to hire a lawyer. They set up an escrow account and asked for donations from the local arts community, and quickly raised a few thousand dollars. They had another meeting with the Department of Revenue, this time in their lawyer's office. The auditor wouldn't shake their hands. Lynette told me he suddenly had a nervous tic in his jaw; Venus said he was furious, shaking, yelling, and she was scared. "To see his reaction at the last meeting . . . you don't want to feel that way with your government. Your government is supposed to be there, supposed to have your back, you know?"

Venus and Lynette were offered the chance to settle with the department for pennies on the dollar, but they declined, as they both would have lost the ability to file as self-employed. Venus told me they had discussed the possibility beforehand, and had agreed not to settle; they saw the money they had already raised as a clear message from the arts community. "We're fighting a fight that's beyond us," she said. "We're not stopping. I don't want the arts community in Minnesota, or anywhere, to be so afraid to call themselves what they are."

After the meeting, they received an official and final determination. The Department of Revenue decided to accept Lynette's Schedule C as filed, reversing its preliminary determination, but it still deemed Venus a hobbyist.

Venus's CV goes back to 1984, when she released her first album. She hasn't always made a profit, and in some years she wrote off extensive losses and got by thanks in part to her wife's income. After the Department of Revenue issued its final determination, she and Lynette owed a total of $3,535, including interest and penalties; more importantly, Venus could no longer claim her art practice as a business or file a Schedule C as self-employed.

For a while after that, things were tough. After a blockage in an artery affectionately nicknamed "the widow maker" caused pain she could no longer ignore, Venus underwent heart surgery while her lawyer began work on an administrative appeal. She and Lynette both struggled to work and to keep up the fight despite the emotional and financial costs, and they rallied after a few months. Lynette got a contract for her first book, and Venus mounted an ambitious performance piece, had a solo exhibition of her drawings, and booked concerts six months out across the country. Without the support of the community, Venus and Lynette would never have been able to fight; their legal fees reached $12,000. Few working artists have those kinds of cash reserves on hand, or the decades of commitment to community that helped Venus and Lynette raise money. When it comes to taxes, as with so many things, the ability to fight belongs to those who can afford it.

No one could tell if the content of Venus's work or anything about her person mattered to the Department of Revenue. These people are Minnesotans, so there's no hyperbole, no accusations. They say they can't tell. But they bring it up out of nowhere, so they probably can tell.

John said he didn't want to be paranoid. "I don't want to use the word 'shocked,' but basically, I don't understand how the conclusion that the state got to, how they got to that," said John. "And are there other outside things going on? Is somebody after him or is it, because Venus is Venus? . . . There isn't any evidence of that. But there isn't any logical reason to me why they came to the conclusion they did, that his efforts are going to be considered a hobby." Lynette apologized for indulging in her "little conspiracy theories" before suggesting that political actors might be attempting to delegitimize the state's significant funding for the arts, that Venus's gender presentation might make some people uncomfortable, that her own position as the family breadwinner might be hard for some to understand. Then she waved away any suggestion of ill intent: "I don't think it's even conscious on their part. I think they just find our situation so unusual, it's something they can't get their head around. For an institution that you would think is based totally on numbers, it's very emotional on their side, I think."[11]

Sometimes the line between professional and amateur is a clear, bright one. But in the United States, artists are, for the most part, just artists, moving in and out of day jobs and commercial work, employment and unemployment, windfall and drought. Professional artist, serious artist, working artist, real artist. Around here, these are fighting words. They mean so much in part because we don't agree—can't agree—on what they mean. In fact, we prefer not to agree, and for our uncertainties we are rewarded with a rich and vibrant cultural life. There are no clear definitions, and absent the occasional obscenity or copyright trial, there are no authorities to enforce the boundaries. The state Departments of Revenue and the Internal Revenue Service end up being, somehow, the only mechanisms the state has to determine an artist's status with any finality. But they do it without the benefit of clear, transparent rules, and in the end, it seems that agents audit people, not their receipts. Both sides try their best to stick to a simple story, but the complex narratives of value that shape the art field transcend individuals, complicating any attempt to arrive at a single indisputable truth. It's the auditor who decides: you're an artist, or maybe you're not. And as Venus told me the first time we spoke, it can crush you.

In the spring of 2014, Venus and her lawyer submitted a request for her auditor's notes. After much back and forth, rather than giving them the notes they requested, the Department of Revenue asked them to come in for a meeting with a new auditor—to make a fresh start. One month later, a year and a half after her audit began, Venus received a notice in the mail. It read, "After reviewing all of the information available, it is our determination that the taxpayer's art/music activity was engaged in for profit as defined under Treasury Regulation 1.183-2." At the back of the letter, she found a check for $70. The department's audit showed that Venus was, after all, owed a small refund.

. . .

In this book, I have sought to understand and explain the ways that artists talk about the value of the things that they do. The patterns I found led me to a concern with commensuration as a social process and to a model of social processes of disagreement about value in working life. But I've closed with this story about Venus and her audit to bring the conversation back to the ground, where I live. When we talk about value, we are never simply talking about money. We're talking about what we do, who we are, and who we want to be.

Methodological Appendix

This is a book about work, and value, and public life. I got interested in those three issues together when I moved from the United States to Sweden in 2003. Back then when I was at a party and someone asked what I did, I would say that I was an artist. When I moved, my working life turned upside down, even though the art objects I made changed relatively little. A lot of my work was about knowledge, classification, and science. For the last big project I did, I spent a couple of years doing research on what it is that artists do: what artistic practice consists of. The point was to create a classification system for that labor, for the everyday activities that artists engage in to produce their work, and then to make an object out of it, one that would be real and not-real at the same time, that would be a sort of prompt. Like a lot of my artwork, it looked a bit like social science. And by the time I was done with it, I felt I had gone as far as I could, that I needed a new tack. So at some point, I decided to become a scientist. Sort of. In 2008, I went back to school, to get a different lens to look through, and entered a PhD program in sociology. Nowadays, I am very much a sociologist, and this is thoroughly a work of sociology. But my experience in art worlds (first in Minnesota, where I'm from originally, and then in Sweden, with time spent working in Austria, Norway, Finland, Iceland, and Macedonia as well) has certainly had immense influence on this study.

During the course of this study, as I spoke with a very diverse sample of artists and spent time in art communities very unlike the ones I was formerly at home in (including many I would not have previously recognized as legitimate art communities at all), I saw very quickly how narrow and specific my own experience had been. Artists I knew from before I began my PhD work have been surprised at my project: "but I haven't seen you around *that* much." They often have real difficulty imagining an art world beyond their own, or at least imagining any that might matter beyond their own; I hear this sort of comment primarily from artists who are embedded in the high contemporary art world, who assume that a study like mine is neither plausible nor interesting without a chapter on Documenta and another on Jeffrey Deitch. In my former life, I was embedded in one subcategory of this world: one that was nonprofit and academically oriented, revolving around art academies and biennials, kunsthalles and quirky museums, international travel and funded residencies in second cities. It was exceedingly metronormative and, in the end, quite small. As an artist, I had far more in common with the academic sociologists that now populate my working life than I did with Land, selling drawings and paintings in local shops, or with Josh, with whom I would have been able to talk easily about artworks but whose experience near the top of the art market would have been entirely foreign to me.

In writing this book, I have returned to my old notebooks from time to time. These notebooks—combination sketchbook, to-do list, diary, calendar, and what I would now call fieldnotes, full of quotes and commentary—are never referred to directly but did serve me on background as a sort of preliminary, naturalistic ethnography, and I hope that this book is richer for my experience "in the field." I have a few short notes on method.

·   ·   ·

The majority of the discussion in this book is drawn from an interview-based study with eighty visual artists. *Visual artists* are defined for this project in terms of *practice*: they are people who have publicly exhibited visual artworks (drawing, painting, sculpture, photographs, and other forms commonly shown in institutions like museums of contemporary art) in the year prior to the interview. This criterion of public exhibition in the past year restricts the study to visual artists who are known, by at least a small public, to be working as artists and minimizes the extent to which practice as a visual artist is a past, fading, or temporarily-on-hold element of the individual's life. This sample is intended to capture artists with varying levels and types of success in multiple art worlds,[1] and is purposively designed as a maximum variation sample.[2] It is based in a definition of practice in order to capture as much diversity in the population of visual artists as possible, and this sample exhibits wide variation along occupational and economic lines, among other dimensions. The sample includes artists working full- and part-time in organizations both in and outside the art world, as well as artists who work on a freelance basis, artists who work for themselves in many forms, and artists with no incomes.

The sample draws on the sites at which art is shown and sold to the public: galleries, museums, art centers, and other presenting institutions. I chose a range intended to capture variation in the types of presenting institutions currently active in the exhibition of visual art in the United States, representing different art worlds, with both regional and urban / rural variation. These presenting institutions included a major contemporary art museum, an artist-run space, a community-based sales gallery, a municipal art gallery, a rural art crawl, an airport, a church. For each presenting institution selected, I constructed a roster of artists who had exhibited or sold artworks through the institution in the past year, and that roster was further narrowed to living artists currently residing in the United States. From this roster at each institution, I selected two to six artists at random to contact for an interview, with nearly all artists contacted agreeing to an interview. I was unable to schedule meetings with three artists, either because they did not want to participate or because we were unable to agree on a time (which may have been due to reluctance on their part). One more was too ill to participate, and died shortly after I asked for an interview. When I was unable to schedule an interview with a particular artist, I chose another at random from the same roster. Twice in my initial random draw, I chose artists I had already met; in these two instances, I chose to draw again rather than carry out interviews with acquaintances. When I guessed that artists might not want to speak with me (because I imagined them to be too famous or too busy), I occasionally engaged intermediaries that I perceived as higher-status than I or who I thought might be common acquaintances to provide an introduction. The resulting sample displays regional and urban/rural diversity beyond the particular institutions from which the rosters were drawn, since (for example) a New York nonprofit art center might exhibit mainly artists from the Northeast and from Los Angeles but a few artists from the hinterlands will also sneak in. The sample represents diversity in occupational commitment and success in the fine arts, education, income level and type, gender, age, race, class background, and other dimensions. This project happened thanks to the generosity of many who helped in so many big and small ways, but three people deserve a particular shout out: Jen Weintraub and Tom Hyry, who not once but twice let me invade their home on research trips and who are the two coolest brarians I know; and Alison Teal, whose home I have also taken shameful advantage of twice in these past years, and whose generosity knows no bounds.

With the exception of William Schaff, who appears in the first chapter, and Venus DeMars and Lynette Reini-Grandell, in chapter seven, none of whom were part of the interview study sample, as well as a few artists and critics whose published writings I discuss in chapter two, I refer to artists only by pseudonyms; I asked all those I interviewed to choose pseudonyms themselves so that they may see themselves in the research, can fact-check my representations and contest my interpretations, can respond if they wish.[3] I cannot thank the artists that I spoke with for this study by name, but I hope that they know how grateful I am for their time, energy, thoughts, and hospitality. I hope that they see themselves in these pages, and that they smile. Venus, Lynette, and Will deserve extra thanks for letting me peek into their lives and put them on the record.

Pilot interviews for this study were carried out as oral history interviews with visual artists, lawyers, consultants, and stay-at-home parents. These served me on background, but they are not included in this study. This study was not designed for quantitative analysis, and does not pretend to approximate a statistically representative sample of all of the visual artists in the United States. Social scientists have a relatively good sense of certain populations of artists, such as those with MFA degrees or those who make most of their income from their artistic work,[4] but the practice-based definition used in this project does not map well onto these previously defined populations, and this study is unique in its reach.

.   .   .

Issues of interview design merit particular discussion. Especially relevant here are issues of direct and indirect questioning. Asking directly about value—"How do you think about the value of your practice?"—is, on its face, a problematic prompt. Debates in economics over contingent valuation show how difficult it can be to interpret what appear to be straightforward accounts of value.[5] I aimed, throughout this study, to design interviews that allowed me to ask about actual events and practices, and I avoided questions that asked in the abstract what a respondent "thought" or (God forbid) "felt" about an issue or concept. In pilot interviews, I found that artists were very ready and able to answer questions about value eloquently and with emphatic "sound bites." I found, too, that these sound bites had very little to do with their descriptions of choices they made, hopes they nurtured, and analyses they offered of others.[6] I do not expect individuals to be internally coherent logicians,[7] but the answers artists offered in these early interviews to abstract questions were generally both unrelated to more concrete questions and unusually practiced and fluent. During this pilot stage, I also carried out interviews with lawyers and consultants. While they also displayed this (very normal) disjuncture between word and deed, their discussions of value rarely struck me as similarly practiced, whereas I found that artists were especially ready to offer sound bites about value.

Based on observation and my own experience of higher education in the arts, my interpretation of this gap is twofold. First, as value in the arts is unusually contentious and ambiguous, artists may be more likely than those in other fields to have a practiced position statement vis-à-vis value. Second, artists, especially those trained in BFA and MFA programs, are likely to be unusually skilled at telling interlocutors what they want to hear: this is a skill that is necessary in the profession and is honed through years of practice. Artists hoping to have their work shown must convince others (curators in particular but also others generally, since one never knows when a loose tie will lead to an opportunity) that the work they've done, generally an object with symbolic content open to interpretation, is unique, exciting, and relevant to the curator, collector, or viewer's *own interests.*

It is this last feature that I am speaking of here; artists learn over time to "read the room," to intuit ways that their work can be positioned discursively in order to speak directly to an interlocutor. This process can be observed directly by watching artists speak to one and then another curator or critic about a single object; artists pick up on cues, expand on them, and discursively mold their objects to fit the interests of the person they're speaking to. One artist, Gregory, spoke to the downfalls of such a skill when he told me why it was, for him, so hard to get meaningful feedback: "Over the years I've become a very good salesman. I'm able to sell people on these different projects and what I think of as what they would like about it; I'm able to portray it that way."

Artists are often able to "sell" the meaning and value of the thing that they've done in a way that's likely to appeal to their interlocutor, just as a shopkeeper might read each customer's carriage and sell a "durable" jacket to one person and the same jacket as "fine" to another, or to use a less emphatically commercial example, just as a pastor will develop a knowledge of her flock's relationships, problems, and dreams in order to speak effectively both to the congregation as a whole and, over cakes afterward and in her office on a Tuesday, to each individual in turn. Relationally aware responses to abstract questions are not either dishonest or unmeaningful, but as I quickly found that they seemed to offer little insight into the issues I was interested in, I chose to ask questions in a different way, beginning with the way I requested an initial meeting with each artist. In my first e-mails, I told artists that I was interested in talking to them about "meaning in working life and contemporary artmaking"—enough to indicate that I was asking for an interview, not a studio visit, yet without directly using terms like *value*. Throughout this research, my strategy has been to ask questions that prompt respondents to tell me stories about concrete things that they have done and are doing. Simply put, my strategy has assumed that people tell you more when they tell you about what they do than when they tell you about what they think.

.   .   .

Transcripts of semistructured interviews are the primary form of data represented here. In keeping with the particular benefits and limitations of interview-based studies, this research aims to understand the experiences of those interviewed, and in particular to understand how individual members of a community of practice[8] that allows for varying levels of occupational commitment and uses of monetary valuation account for the value of their activities and experiences. Interviews were designed with theory-driven prompts, and the interview schedule was occasionally updated inductively, though most questions were retained to allow direct comparability. I carried out all interviews in person; pilot interviews in person, by telephone, and using video chat had shown me that interviews in person were superior for the nature of the questions asked in this study: in-person interviews were on average more than twice as long as interviews by telephone or video chat; they resulted in richer, more wide-ranging data; and they allowed the collection of much more observational data, as they generally took place in the respondent's home or workplace. These taped interviews lasted, on average, 1.75 hours each; were carried out between 2011 and 2013; and were transcribed verbatim and in full and integrated with fieldnotes; I have worked largely from these transcripts. Throughout this book, artist's words enclosed in quotation marks are direct quotes from transcripts of taped material; artist's words not so enclosed, as in my discussion of a visit to William Schaff's studio in chapter one, are my reconstruction from fieldnotes rather than a direct quote. I have made occasional small changes to quotes for readability and confidentiality—including condensing some quotes without supplying ellipses to indicate omissions—but have chosen for the most part to preserve the specificities, disfluencies, and vernacular of spoken language.

I collected career histories, current CVs, and other potentially relevant data. In the context of the interview as much observational data as possible was gathered and documented; I also made fieldnotes on relevant experiences that I engaged in throughout the study (attendance at art exhibitions, for example), both under the assumption that such data would be of value and with the knowledge that such experiences would influence my interpretation of the data.[9] Notes were written or dictated directly after each interview on the interview setting, tone and mood, and other tacit elements, and included preliminary analysis. My fieldnotes for this study, not including interview transcripts, reached 380,000 words, and are represented here when, for example, the setting of an interview is described.

I used an interview schedule for semistructured interviews with all respondents in this study. When possible, the questions were not asked directly as prompts, except in the case of the first question. An ideal interview, for me, proceeded from that first question relatively naturally, and through conversation I found answers to each of the questions in my schedule. When I did not, I asked the relevant questions in turn, using the wordings in my schedule—something that happened very rarely by the end, as I gained experience. My first question was almost always worded exactly as in the schedule ("When you meet someone new and they ask, 'What do you do?' how do you answer?"), as was my last question ("What am I not asking?"). Very few of the questions in the middle were ever asked directly and in turn, however. When artists talked about objects they had made, I asked about the feedback they had received; when they told me about studio assistants and students, I asked what they hoped to teach their pupils. Most interviews proceeded, I hope, as conversations, and I avoided stilted question-answer sessions as much as possible. I saved any abstract questions I might have for the end of the interview, and was interested in the answers mainly as they might give me access to each artist's understanding of currently hegemonic frames for action, or perhaps of the artist's assumptions about my interests. I modified the schedule slightly between the first and last interviews.[10]

In parts of this book, notably in chapter two, I also make use of archival material. A first archival source involves materials relating to artist-activists engaged in conversations about artists' labor, work, and remuneration. I use interpretive analysis of public statements made by individual visual artists on the topic of the artist as worker, often as advocacy related to artists' grassroots organizations and unions, from 1967 through 2015, in three national contexts. I chose to look at artists in the United States, Canada, and Sweden in order to represent a range of welfare states and organizational strategies; I aimed with this cross-national context to bracket issues of local concern. These texts represent a transnational conversation in contemporary artmaking, and their authors argue that they speak for artists generally, whether those authors are members of an artists' organization or not. I began with data from 1967 in order to capture a wave of activity in and around formal and informal organizations beginning in that year and continuing through approximately 1971. This time period is important in both in practical and art historical terms, including the rise and fall of the Art Workers' Coalition (AWC) in New York City, the development of Canadian Artists' Representation (CAR/CARFAC), and major changes in the leadership and direction of the Swedish Artists' National Organization (KRO).

A second source of historical data is a database of 911 oral histories with visual artists, drawn from the Smithsonian's Archives of American Art (all transcribed interviews available from the archive when I constructed the database). These data were intended to complement data on the AWC and contemporary data on Working Artists and the Greater Economy (W.A.G.E.) and to serve as a bridge between archival data focused on artists' organizations and my own interview data, which informs the bulk of this study. The oral histories in the database include interviews dating from the 1950s and later, and I draw on two subsets in particular. The first one consists of artists born in the 1930s and interviewed during the 1960s and '70s; these artists were born in the same decade as many of those recorded as speaking to and for the AWC, and were interviewed during the rise and fall of that collective. A second subset of artists is made up of those born after 1960 and interviewed after 2000. They are intended to be comparable both with those artists who are recorded as speaking for W.A.G.E. and the younger artists I have interviewed. The comparative structure in the historical discussions in this book, then, is a T1/T2 comparison, with T1 data consisting of AWC, CAR, and KRO documents as well as oral histories from artists born in the 1930s who were interviewed during the 1960s and '70s, and T2 data consisting of W.A.G.E., KRO, IKK,[11] and CARFAC documents, oral histories from artists born after 1960 and interviewed after 2000, and my own interviews and participant observation (2008 and later). Analyses from archival sources are drawn on in the discussions of diachronic processes, while my own interviews provide the basis for the synchronic processes I outline.

.   .   .

In my analyses, I used the constant comparative method[12] but with a commitment to the abductive approach outlined by Timmermans and Tavory.[13] Constant comparison allowed me to reduce the mass of empirical detail into manageable categories and clusters of categories, each made up of words, ideas, and narratives that shared specific qualities. I returned to the data again and again, slowly developing categories as discussed below, and allowing those categories to be born, expand, contract, multiply, marry, and sometimes die as my understanding of the patterns I saw in the data developed. By *abductive*, I mean that I depart from grounded theory's insistence that the analyst approach the data without subjectivity or theory. I began this study with deep background knowledge of lay and technical theories of value in the arts, both from my past artistic practice in a relatively academic setting and from my engagement with sociological works on the value of art and artmaking. This informed my development of a research question as well as the first wave of coding. I did not approach the data with an empty mind. Like Timmermans and Tavory, I don't think that other researchers do either, nor do I think that pretending we do is the best way to build theory. Throughout the analysis, I continued to work with the data, to read widely, and to discuss initial findings with academic, professional, and artistic colleagues.

Writing and using fieldnotes was my first form of analysis. A detailed record of the project as a whole was kept, including notes on correspondence with respondents and others, detailed memos on interviews and their settings, preliminary analysis of interviews, notes on informal conversations and participant observation data, relevant archival and secondary source material, and reflective and analytical writings. These fieldnotes allowed me to see how and when lines of inquiry arose and to note objects of interest that could not yet be integrated into the study's theoretical framework.

In my first wave of coding, I read and reread data looking for recurrent themes. This wave began concurrently with data collection and continued for approximately two and a half years. I aimed to move from individual accounts to a more abstract, theoretically informed account of the field under consideration, and hoped to contribute to current research as well as to present my respondents with a novel but not entirely foreign perspective on their own accounts. During this wave of coding, I moved constantly between the data, an emerging structure of typologies and theoretical arguments, and the literature. As I identified themes in the data and used new data to judge the veracity of the codes I developed and my definitions for inclusion, my codebook expanded and contracted. One early version from this wave included 34 codes and 133 subcodes in families. These codes included such items as "primary identity," "art and effort," and "prices"; the subcodes included such specifications as (for the prices code) "reasonable/fair," "equations," "inherent value," and "hourly wages." I read through the data, added new data as I conducted additional interviews, and read through the data again. I used the themes I saw to integrate new data into an expanding system of codes and used new data to constantly reconsider previously identified codes, to expand or split them, and to abandon codes that did not capture sufficiently widespread or relevant themes.[14] When data, once revisited, did not seem to fit codes I had developed, those codes were either abandoned or revised. Very few of the early codes and subcodes survived intact to the second wave of coding, but a path from each can be traced to the codebook used at the beginning of wave 2, which included 8 codes and 13 subcodes. It included codes such as "speculative" and "credentialing," with specifications (as with the subcodes for credentialing) such as "teaching" and "commercial work." I also coded entire transcripts with demographic and other categorical qualities, beginning with a theoretically informed group of categories (gender, age, class background). These categories also expanded and contracted over time as new data or theory required, with new categories being added throughout the analysis (as with the category "studio outside of home," added midway through, or "earns over half of household income through art work (100% if living alone)," added well into wave two of coding).

I began the second wave of coding as I began to write up my research, now with codes much more abstract than those in the initial codebooks. Before beginning the second wave, I had examined my codes, looking for underlying dimensions that could show how they might fit together into a coherent whole. Throughout my second round of coding, I constantly moved back and forth between my emerging framework and the data that sometimes confirmed, sometimes denied my suppositions. I continued to expand and contract categories, to add and abandon codes. I also refined the typology presented here in chapters three and four.[15]

As this book has moved through several drafts, the number of voices that come through strongly has waxed and waned. As I am looking to abstract from the individual, my goal is, of course, not to represent each individual artist that I spoke with in all of their complexity, but the balance between overwhelming the reader with repetitive evidence and not providing enough evidence has been, I think, hard to strike. If twenty people said the same thing, I chose the quote that I felt best represented all twenty statements; this means that, in the end, a few artists—those who I felt were more articulate, who seemed to have rhetorical skill, who told stories I enjoyed—are overrepresented in these pages. I worked from transcripts for most of this process, but as I finished up this book I returned to the recordings, and listened again to the artists who are quoted little or not at all in this book, looking for things I had missed and things that didn't yet make sense. This process also reminded me, years after the interviews took place and with a texture and depth that the transcripts had lost, how generous all of these artists were to take the time to speak with me, and how grateful I am for their stories and their thoughts.

Notes

Chapter 1. Art Work?

1. Here is a simple measure of this rise: the economic sociology section of the American Sociological Association, formed in 2001, had 748 members at the end of 2015, a year when the median number of members per section was 484. In the past decade, in the United States and northern Europe at least, economic sociology has become a legitimate subdiscipline.

2. In one telling, known as "Parsons's Pact," sociologists left value decades ago to economics in order to justify their own authority over the study of values (Stark 2009).

3. See, for example, Tversky and Kahneman 1974, 1981.

4. For an overview, see Zelizer 2011.

5. Almeling 2007; Anteby 2010; Healy 2004.

6. Bandelj 2012; Spillman 1999; Wherry 2008.

7. Wherry 2008.

8. A few economists, though, do illuminate such processes and even argue for them; see, for example, Schor 2010 and Schor et al. 2016.

9. For example, Jerolmack and Khan 2014; Pugh 2013; Vaisey 2014.

10. In this, I follow in the path of other scholars who have worked with the intersection of art and value (e.g., Cowen and Tabarrok 2000; Graw 2010; Velthuis 2003). I look to visual artists to consider whether and how occupationalization affects valuation in a community of practice (Wenger 1998). The practice of visual art is a rich source for those interested in value and valuation. The history of social scientific analysis in the visual arts has been one in which our collective attention has shifted from a strict interest in (cultural) values to a broader view that includes (economic) value. Contemporary research displays a central interest in price (Cowen and Tabarrok 2000; Fine 2003; Menger 2001, 2014), while sustaining a sense that pricing in the arts is ill captured by neoclassical economic theory (Karpik 2010; Velthuis 2005). Such lack of fit has fuelled critiques of commodification as well as models explaining constraints on it and modifications to circulation protocols (Kopytoff 1986;

Wherry 2006). However, in its focus on art objects, such research largely neglects artistic practice, and the assumption of a fundamental mismatch between market value and aesthetic value has led to a focus on problems of commodification that can just as well be understood as issues of valuation for the analyst less committed to a hostile worlds framework (Zelizer 2000). An approach that considers artistic practice as a whole—a field encompassing both wholly marketized and entirely non-commodified practices—allows for a clearer image of historical and contemporary artistic practice and at the same time refigures questions of market value as questions about the appropriate valuation of practice rather than about the appropriate status of objects.

While I use valuation in the arts as a lens for thinking about working life outside of the arts as well, I of course draw on the strong tradition in sociology that treats the arts and artists as objects of study worth our consideration; I am thinking, for example, of Crane 1989; Fine 2003; White and White 1965; and Zolberg 1990 and especially Becker 1982, from which I draw heavily in my conceptualization of "art worlds."

11. This emphasis on practices differentiates my work from much of the literature in economic sociology on valuation; Zelizer, for example, looks at childhood with a treatment that considers not parenting practices nor the experience of childhood but the value of children as sort-of objects (Zelizer 1981). My emphasis on practice is a departure in this literature. In my own perspective on art pricing, I depend in particular on Olav Velthuis's account; his attention to gift and honor economies strikes me as crucial for understanding fields like contemporary art as well as generative for thinking about valuation in other, less obviously creative fields (Velthuis 2005). In my perspective on the valuation of cultural objects more generally, I rely on Clayton Childress's work on novels and the institutions that contribute to their production and reception, owing to that work's attention to the relationships between high-culture actors, organizations, and cultural structures (Childress 2017).

12. To whatever extent talk is considered a fundamental element of our relationship to objects (e.g., Foucault 1972), modern art has long been understood to be intimately tied up with language. Harold Rosenberg wrote in the 1970s that a "contemporary painting or sculpture is a species of centaur—half art materials, half words"; many critics today would argue that the words have won (Princenthal 2013; Rosenberg 1972).

Chapter 2. The Work of Art

1. Art Workers' Coalition 1969a:102–110.
2. Art Workers' Coalition 1969b:38.
3. Lozano 2009.
4. Steiner 2008.
5. While practices that look much like modern jobs can be found in antiquity, contemporary sociological research on occupations and work tends, like Weber, to

trace the shape of modern occupational employment to processes of bureaucratization and rationalization and to see working life as central to life in capitalism and
to democratic participation (Goldberg 2007; Weber 2001). Professionalization—one
mode of occupational development—is of particular interest here. While research in
the professions literature on other occupations is often concerned with the boundaries of the professional category (Abbott 1988; Brante 2011; Evetts 2003; Freidson 1986;
Saks 2012; Wilensky 1964), much can be gained through the adoption of a professions lens to investigate a particular (apparently nonprofessional) occupational field's
theory and practice. Rich and generative studies in the professions tradition include
Larson's analysis of the political ramifications of new markets in professional services
(Larson 1977), Spillman's investigation into the professional side of apparently non-
professional work (Spillman 2012), Berman's study of the organizational and intra-
professional dynamics of professionalization processes (Berman 2006), and Timmermans's ethnography of professional authority and autonomy (Timmermans 2005).

6. Political work, another example, can be done by unpaid volunteers with PhDs
in political science or well-paid advisors with backgrounds in advertising; there are
few barriers to running for office and no limit to the demands on elected officials
despite some full-timers being paid only in parking passes while others with fewer
responsibilities earn good full-time salaries.

7. Bourdieu (1984) and those writing in the rich tradition following his outline
relationships between distinction and economic, social, and cultural capital. For discussions of these processes in art worlds, see, for example, Banks 2012; Battani 1999;
Becker 1982; Entwistle 2002; and Wilson 2007.

8. On historical practice, see, for example, Gordon 2006; Kemp 1997; Montias
1989; Vasari 1987; White and White 1965; Wittkower and Wittkower 2007.

9. Baxandall 1972; Haynes 1997; O'Malley 2005.

10. Baxandall 1972:1. I will follow Baxandall in this chapter, and refer to those
we might otherwise think of as "commissioners," "collectors," or "patrons" as *clients*.

11. O'Malley 2005.

12. On the clients' side of things, and in particular the visibility and effects of
"conspicuous commissions," see Nelson and Zeckhauser 2008.

13. Friedenthal 1963:16.

14. Goldwater and Treves 1945:145–46.

15. Friedenthal 1963:58.

16. Haynes 1997.

17. Baxandall 1972; Bryan-Wilson 2009; Haynes 1997; O'Malley 2005; Roberts
2007.

18. Burwick 2001; Roberts 2007. While the ideas appear to have come from philosophical discussions in the decade prior, the first recorded use of the phrase comes
from an 1804 note by Benjamin Constant on philosophical aesthetics. For primers on
the history of art for art's sake see, for example, Burwick 2014 and Jenkins 1973. The

phrase is usually taken to be primarily an aesthetic and moral argument, but its economic causes and consequences are clear. On these, see, for example, Guérard 1936.

19. "Art for Art's Sake" 1917; Bell-Villada 1986; Guérard 1936; Singer 1954; Wilcox 1953. Remnants of art-for-art's sake thinking can of course be seen everywhere today coexisting with other visions of artistic identity and practice, as will be discussed below.

20. See, for example, the 1932 Draft Manifesto of the John Reed Club of New York: "we call upon all honest intellectuals, all honest writers and artists, to abandon decisively the treacherous illusion that art can exist for art's sake, or that the artist can remain remote from the historic conflicts in which all men must take sides. . . . We call upon them to align themselves with the working class in its struggle against capitalist oppression and exploitation" (Harrison and Wood 2003:421).

21. For further reading on the Federal Art Project, see, for example, Monroe 1972, 1974; and O'Connor 1969. The oft-cited number—10,000 artists employed—is somewhat misleading, as many of the funded projects were closer to folk art, craft, or community development enterprises than the fine art purchase and production schemes we most often remember.

22. For an on-the-ground view of the experience of the Art Project see, for example, Solomon 2001 on Jackson Pollock and his circle in the 1930s.

23. Hess 1962, cited in Elderfield 2011:55.

24. Bryan-Wilson 2009.

25. Yup.

26. I turned to the archives to find out what the rationalization of artistic practice meant—why it mattered, and what had changed. I found texts written far afield that were reprinted in American newsletters and also other evidence that this rationalization was a cross-national phenomenon; further, the more I dug into the archives, the more I was distracted by issues of only local concern and personality conflicts among artists that played out in public. I decided to focus on one set of discussions—conversations about remuneration, about getting paid—and to look at these discussions across three national contexts. This made it easier to bracket out local variation and to highlight broadly shared cultural structures. I chose three countries to focus on: Sweden, Canada, and the United States. These contexts were selected using Esping-Andersen's (1990) typology of states in order to include variation along the dimension of direct state intervention in the arts as an element of the welfare state. In the liberal United States, individual artists have little hope of ever receiving funding directly from the state for their work; in Canada, somewhat more is available, along with other forms of social insurance that influence artists' careers; while in social democratic Sweden, individual artists can expect direct state intervention in their careers and art markets generally. By way of example, compare the National Endowment for the Arts in the United States with Konstnärsnämnden, the Swedish Arts Grants Committee. In 2015 in the

United States (population 318 million), fifty artists in total received $25,000 awards from the NEA (National Endowment for the Arts 2016a, 2016b, 2016c, 2016d). That year in Sweden (population 9.6 million), if we look only to the awards most similar to those awarded by the NEA (*arbetsstipendium* and *projektbidrag*), 617 individual artists received awards averaging $14,000 (Konstnärsnämnden 2016a, 2016b). While in the United States only an elite few ever hope to receive NEA funds directly and artists cannot count on such funds, in the Swedish context, essentially all working artists have either received such funds or are closely acquainted with artists who have (although see Gerber and Childress, 2017b, for *indirect* state intervention in the U.S. case).

27. The rest of this chapter draws on two bodies of historical data to investigate change over time: archival and secondary sources concerning artists' collectives and oral history interviews with visual artists. "Sources concerning artists' collectives" refers to my database of public statements made by American, Canadian, and Swedish visual artists engaged in some form of advocacy for artists as workers since 1967, with special attention to conversations taking place around five organizations: Canadian Artists' Representation, the Art Workers' Coalition, Working Artists and the Greater Economy, the Swedish Artists' National Organization, and the Institute for Artists and Art Mediators. These organizations serve as sites of extensive and focused longitudinal discussions about art as work and issues of remuneration. "Oral history interviews with visual artists" refers to a body of 911 oral histories with visual artists from the Smithsonian Institution's Archives of American Art. See the appendix for more information on the oral histories, newsletters, and other texts referred to in this chapter and for discussions of change over time; my own interviews and observations provide the basis for the rest of this book, and are also considered in more detail in the appendix.

28. See, for example, Conner 1974.

29. Amos 1968.

30. Frutkin 1987:2.

31. LeWitt 1969:54.

32. Chambers, Ondaatje, and Urquhart 1973:2.

33. Chambers 1973:38; Perreault 1969:120; Tateishi 1985:4.

34. Gordy 1969:98.

35. LeWitt 1969:54.

36. These goals have since been attained to various degrees, most notably in Canada where the "exhibition right" was made law and moral rights were significantly expanded in 1987.

37. Suttner 1971a:9.

38. Petré 1981:4.

39. Amundson 1982:10.

40. James 1978:7.

41. Beveridge 2005:5.

42. This shift parallels real changes in Western economies away from manufacturing and toward growth in the service sector; the changes identified here are likely part of a general shift toward valuation of time rather than tangible production. Organisation for Economic Co-operation and Development (OECD) Labour Force Statistics report that, in 2008, 79.5% of civilian employment in the United States was in services, compared to 58.1% in 1960; these statistics also show that "the services sector now accounts for over 70% of total employment and value added in OECD economies. It also accounts for almost all employment growth in the OECD area" (OECD 2005). For an excellent discussion of some of the ramifications of valuing products versus valuing time, see Biernacki 1995.

43. Chambers 1973:38.

44. Yates 1983:2.

45. Beveridge, 2005: 4–5.

46. Suttner 1971a:7, 1971b:5.

47. Ewald 2002:1.

48. Nordwall 2005:6.

49. Fraser 1997:112.

50. Working Artists and the Greater Economy 2016.

51. Mondini-Ruiz 2004.

52. Graw 2010. See also Relyea 2013 for an exploration of the ways that project, site-specific, platform, and other post-studio practices simultaneously resist, reinscribe, and reinvent capitalist dynamics and gallery-artist relationships.

53. Hardy 2008.

54. Backman et al. 2006.

55. Equivalent to about 33 million U.S. dollars in January 2017.

56. Reichert, Backman, and Palm, 2007.

57. Nguyen 2009.

58. Bain 2005; Otterman 2014.

59. With the exception of William Schaff in chapter one, Venus De Mars in chapter seven, and the artists and critics whose published writings I discuss in this chapter, I refer to artists by first names only, pseudonyms they chose themselves.

60. Of course, to be included in the population of artists I aimed to speak with, an artist needed to have exhibited artwork in the past year in some way. Today, most artists define occupational status in relation to public exhibition, however humble or infrequent—not, as one might expect, in terms of credentials, employers, income, or other markers of a job. Public exhibition is an important element of the performance of commitment, of serious art practice. There are, of course, artists who proudly consider themselves hobbyists, amateurs, Sunday painters; I imagine that they simply don't exhibit much when art worlds demand at least a professional pose. Thanks most likely to the exhibition-focused way that I chose the artists who

are represented in these pages, artists who proudly call themselves amateurs or don't identify as "real" artists don't appear in this study. I have of course met and spent time with artists who don't fit the occupationalized mold that I have laid out here, but they are relatively few and far between and, I would argue, wander so far from the norm in so many different directions that I cannot do justice to their diversity here. I have discussed this in earlier writing (Gerber 2014b) on bad art as calisthenics for social engagement. I expected at least some artists that I met thanks to exhibitions in what might be considered lower-status institutions—suburban coffee shops or church foyers, for example—to consider themselves hobbyists, but this was not the case. Land was representative in her understanding of the difference between "real" art practice and the rest; she told me that the first question she got when she said she was a painter was whether she was "serious about it" or not. When I asked her to clarify what she meant by "serious," she responded: "I think they mean more as in, whether I do it just for my own enjoyment and don't actually show it out, or whether I actually am going out canvassing for places to show."

61. Gregory Sholette has a useful discussion of value and the oversupply of artists as an enduring feature of art worlds in *Dark Matter* (Sholette 2010). On a related process in another field, see Mears 2011.

62. For example, Davis 2013; Gan et al. 2014; Halperin 2012; Jahoda et al. 2014; Martin 2011; Reilly 2015; Saltz 2007; Strategic National Arts Alumni Project 2013.

63. Singerman 1999.

64. For example, Berner, House, and Warren 2013; Rubinstein 2007.

65. For example, Remington 1973.

66. Singerman 1999:6.

67. On this, see Gerber and Childress, 2017a.

68. See, for example, Bain (2005) on how important the notion of professionalism is to "serious" artistic practice and identity.

69. Abbott 1981, 1983, 1988; Berman 2006; Brain 1991; Childress and Gerber 2015; Chua and Clegg 1990; Freidson 1986, 2001; Larson 1977; Revers 2013; Spillman 2012; Timmermans 2005.

70. Solomon 2001.

Chapter 3. Making Cents of Art

1. The standard 50/50 artist / dealer split on the sale price is so normalized that Josh doesn't explain it, assuming that I will understand what he means when he says, "each one will sell for $15,000, which means that I will make $7,500 for each."

2. Shapira 2014.

3. Menger 1999; Towse 1996.

4. This strategy, one we trace back to Weber's ideal types (*ideal* as in *ideas*, not as in best: Weber 1949, 2001), assumes that abstracting from the data aids in theorizing, especially through the comparisons it makes possible; with pattern recognition I aim

to produce abstractions that are good to think with. See, for example, the ways that typification is used in Aspers 2009; Evans, Kunda, and Barley 2004; and Mears 2015. The typology presented here is contextually and historically specific, as I discuss below. Ideal-typical analysis is at its best when in the service of something larger, and when done without too much respect for typifications built from faraway times and places (Adams 2005).

5. There are, of course, other ways to think about art markets—among other things, they might expand, bringing in ever larger publics, a tide lifting all boats. The pecuniary account, though, never acknowledges such possibilities.

6. Snyder 2013, 2016.

7. Weber 1978.

8. Biernacki 1995.

9. At times, the ways some artists spoke about their temperament as a kind of credential seemed to fit a particularly modern and individualist worldview about the place of credentials in a labor market: it's not just that artmaking gives you separable and modular skills that have value, they seemed to say; rather, it's that they were people who as individuals had value, a value that was honed with and within artistic practice but that may have been there all along. They just had, they said, the right attitude.

10. For a similar process in another field, see Childress 2012.

Chapter 4: Making Sense of Art

1. Bunderson and Thompson 2009; Wrzesniewski and Dutton 2001.

2. Caves 2003.

3. For a discussion of a similar process in another field, see Plummer 2002.

4. Thompson 1967.

5. Rosso, Dekas, and Wrzesniewski 2010; Wrzesniewski et al. 1997.

6. While these notions might seem hopelessly naïve to a Bourdieusian, there are other perspectives we might draw from: see, for example, Coleman 2016.

7. One way to think about these dynamics is to look at the groups that form thanks to these artistic relationships as "collaborative circles" (Farrell 2001) in which friendships contribute to innovative creative work. If that is so, perhaps artists who self-consciously promote relational values and engage in the kinds of institution-building and long-term conversation that often result enjoy privileged access to some creative processes.

8. Polanyi 2001.

9. For example, Leijonhielm 1987.

10. Bishop 2004:65–69.

11. Bourriaud 2002; Lacy 1995.

12. Finkelpearl 2000:5.

13. Harding 1997:17–18.

14. Carnegie Mellon University 2014.

15. California College of the Arts 2014.

16. The art field points us toward a set of hypotheses about the institutionalization of new accounts. It also suggests that instrumental, measurable, and objective outcomes will vary along with the diverse accounts of value.

17. Espeland and Stevens 1998.

18. An illustration from the literature will clarify what I mean by "social studies of commensuration." In a comparative study of oil spills that affected coastlines in the United States and France, Marion Fourcade showed how different understandings of nature—its value and uses, its "nature"—in the two countries led to very different outcomes. Victims of the spill were conceptualized differently, for example: in France, local users of the shoreline were the victims that counted, whereas in the United States, the American public as a whole was seen to have been affected. French experts estimated the price of the biomass destroyed in spills, while American experts calculated the subjective value to American individuals of the environment spoiled in the spill. Fourcade showed how, in both countries, natural coastlines were understood and reinscribed as "priceless" by economic, scientific, and technical institutions, but she also found that in the United States, "priceless" was worth a whole lot more than in France. The *Exxon Valdez* spill in Alaska led to payouts of over $3 billion, whereas the *Amoco Cadiz* spill in Brittany, at six times the size, resulted in total payouts of just $200 million (Fourcade 2011). How we define the value of nature—the cultural resources we draw on in order to come to a dollar value—matters, and in this case, valuation done in two different ways led to two distinct outcomes. This despite the fact that, of course, the two incidents were not isolated; the people involved could have learned from one another, one simply importing the other's model.

19. I thank an anonymous reviewer for suggesting this framing, and specifically the contrast with Espeland and Stevens's definition of commensuration as the transformation of qualities into quantities (Espeland and Stevens 1998).

Chapter 5: This Way Be Monsters

1. As this chapter and the next will show, the landscapes of value we find in today's art worlds differ in significant ways from those that sociologists would expect to see given assumptions drawn from the central work of Bourdieu (1984, 1985, 1993). I engage in particular with the literature on orders of worth developed from work by Boltanski and Thévenot (1999), and my concerns with that literature—its emphasis on secondary sources and lack of engagement with power and individual agency, as discussed below—are also, in the main, issues that I find in my reading of Bourdieu as well, and serve in part to explain differences in our arguments. Here, though, I will compare a model implied by my work with Bourdieu's to point out the ways that our visions of the art world differ. I engage more directly with Bourdieusian issues

in my work together with Clayton Childress (e.g., Childress and Gerber 2015; Gerber and Childress 2017; Gerber and Childress, 2017a, 2017b).

Bourdieu's model of the art field, one that is appealing in both its simplicity and power, is one that he draws as a straightforward two-dimensional space with two axes. On the x-axis, a continuum between two poles—the *h*eteronomous pole, where art is made for the commercial market, and the *a*utonomous pole, where art is made for art's sake—defines the central tension of art worlds. Artworks (and by extension, artists), then, are more or less autonomous from the field of power, and along the x-axis they are in the main locked into positional and dispositional space. The y-axis demarcates the degree of consecration, and artists' strategies concern ladder-climbing up the y-axis toward more consecration, success, the right kind of audience. Because the model is dualistic, it suggests that good-evil dichotomies are intrinsic to the field, and it allows for purity of orientation, focus, and identity as artists and artworks are positioned farther out from the center along the x-axis. This model is powerful and certainly allows for a satisfying system of classification: for example, an artwork is more or less difficult to understand; we place it on the autonomous pole and assume its maker aims for a small intellectual audience, even that sales would pollute its standing. The model's parsimony, in particular, is beguiling. But however well this model may describe the market positions of some art *objects*, its analytical leverage on the broader art field—one made up of diverse multiple and overlapping art worlds populated by agentic actors who only sometimes made those objects, and only sometimes for that market—is today lacking.

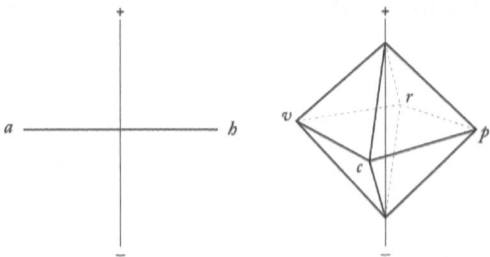

The four types of account described in chapters three and four, and the ways these types interact, explored in this chapter and the next, create a landscape of value with a structure unlike that proposed by Bourdieu, one that involves different gravitational forces. If artists and artworks navigate the coordinates of a flat plane in Bourdieu's work, then in a first sketch of the arguments in this book they populate and navigate a field in three dimensions: an octahedron with Bourdieu's y-axis running through the center of its base. This three-dimensional space is simultaneously aesthetic, relational, and interactional; any agreements regarding a given object's, individual's, or practice's position are necessarily temporary and contingent (this is more true of the objects in Bourdieu's model than Bourdieu is normally given credit for as well). A distinction between the ways artists navigate this kind of three-dimensional space and Bourdieu's graph is the relative value of purity. In Bourdieu's model, an excess of autonomy—going too far down the art-for-art's sake road—is dangerous, of course, for the heteronomous-pole artist, but only solidifies the autonomous-pole artist's commitment; the only danger is to that artist's wallet. In my sketch, though, the four types of account discussed here (*vocational*, *pecuniary*, *credentialing*, *relational*) must be negotiated simultaneously by artists and artworks that hope for legitimacy of any kind; too much autonomy here runs the risk of leaving (or being shut out of) the art world entirely. The vertices that mark the outermost points on the base don't represent goals or pure figures; they are, instead, the caricatures that mark the boundaries of legitimate artistic practice, each of them a cautionary tale.

2. Most of the artists I spoke with followed the kinds of lifestyle promoted by low-growth and degrowth economists (e.g., Schor 2010).

3. Daniels 1985; Luxton 1980; Messias et al. 1997; Wright 1995. The social dominance and legibility of economic and market logics is surely not true in all contexts, and may in its particular contours be specifically American; comparative work on evaluation and valuation illuminates the significant differences the analyst might find in a different context (see, e.g., Fourcade 2011 for an instance and Lamont 2012 for an overview of the field).

4. Disch and O'Brien 2007; Hochschild 1997. For a contemporary look at the ways today's ideal worker shapes our minds and lives, see Pugh 2015.

5. Becher 2014.

6. For example, Boltanski and Thévenot 2006; Freidson 2001; Ruef and Scott 1998; Thornton and Ocasio 1999; Thornton 2001.

7. For example, Anteby 2010; Aspers 2009; Childress 2012; Franssen and Kuipers 2013; Healy 2006; Spillman 1999.

8. Boltanski and Thévenot 2006.

9. Stark 2009.

10. Think, for example, of Vantablack and its controversies (Voon 2016).

Chapter 6: Doing Things with Words

1. Hyde 1983.

2. Some of my assumptions also came from my reading of the work of Boltanski and Thévenot (2006). To speak bookishly, my engagement with Boltanski and Thévenot revolves around an element of their theory of diverse orders of worth that does not seem to hold in the case under consideration here. In the chapters thus far, I have critiqued the assumption of logical coherence visible in their work, as well as in other work on institutional logics of action, and the argument that "compromises" between apparently incompatible accounts must be "fragile." I do this, first, by showing that in the art community, some such compromises and their patterns

of use are apparently stable and widespread and appear to be deployed to specific ends. Second, I suggest that Boltanski and Thévenot's emphasis on logical coherence is based on a misapprehension of their data's contextual specificity; that is the focus of this chapter.

3. While this assertion does something in particular for this argument, the insight is obviously not a new one. Socrates points out, in Plato's *Phaedrus*, the ways that the written word, the public speech, and the conversation differ from one another: he argues that written texts, in their stability, limit us in our quest for wisdom in important ways. He says that speeches are no better: "You would imagine that they [the speakers] had intelligence, but if you want to know anything and put a question to one of them, the speaker always gives one unvarying answer" (Plato 1892).

4. Importantly, I would argue that they aimed to make sense together with me, rather than to gain something from me. I was, at this point, far enough removed from any active art-world role that it was clear to those I spoke with that I could do little for them, and in almost all cases, we were able to avoid the studio-visit conversations that accompany the presence of anyone with power—the power to network, to show, to sell. Chapters three and four in this book represent these aiming-to-make-sense discussions, while the conversations represented in chapter two are, it should be clear, very different; they aim outward, to a public, and as such are more coherent, more straightforward, and often oriented to gain.

5. Smith 2005.

6. Ciofalo and Traverso 1994; Day and Golan 2005; Golan 2010; Harp, Bachmann, and Loke 2014; The OpEd Project 2012; Woods 2015.

7. The term *order of worth* is drawn from Boltanski and Thevenot's work (Boltanski and Thévenot 2006; see also Heinich 1996; Stark 2009). While their work resonates the most strongly with my data, another way to think about these "orders" would be to look instead to the institutional logics literature; this would draw our attention further toward the public sphere, discussed most clearly here in chapter five (Friedland and Alford 1991; Thornton and Ocasio 1999). Another set of terms would carry this discussion in the direction of Swidler's *tool kit*, and then might recast the occupationalization I trace in chapter two as an unsettled period (Swidler 1986).

8. Akerlof and Kranton 2010; Cobble 1999.

9. Goldberg 2007; Moorhouse 1987; Weber 2001.

10. Fine 1996; Grusky and Weeden 2001; Wright 1995.

11. Messias et al. 1997.

12. Hochschild 2003.

13. Daniels 1987.

14. Daniels 1985; Luxton 1980; Messias et al. 1997; Wright 1995.

15. Evans, Kunda, and Barley 2004; Fischl 2004; Star and Strauss 1999.

16. For an overview of these processes and some sense of their impact on workers, a good place to begin might be Smith 1997.

Chapter 7: The Audit of Venus

Earlier versions of this writing on Venus and her audit appeared in *Narratively* magazine and in the *Berkeley Journal of Sociology*, licensed under CC BY-NC-ND 4.0 (Gerber 2014a, 2014c). I am grateful to both publications, and especially to Brendan Spiegel and David Showalter, for their editorial expertise and for their forward-looking intellectual property policies.

1. This persists despite the likelihood of changing careers among younger cohorts and remains colored by the demanding cash economies in which the "do what you love" ideology really means, always, "do what you love as a job, for money, or you're not really doing it." For another perspective on this see, for example, Tokumitsu 2014.

2. For example, Karttunen 1998; Lena and Lindemann 2014; Menger 2001.

3. Bain 2005.

4. Brooks 2002.

5. Weber 1978.

6. Weber 1968:216.

7. For example, Tversky and Kahneman 1974.

8. Perrow 1979:28.

9. Warhol 1991.

10. For an overview, see Zelizer 2011.

11. I reached out to the Minnesota Department of Revenue, but because they cannot comment on individual cases, they sent me only official boilerplate— "taxpayers expect the Department of Revenue to maintain the confidentiality of their information and we take that responsibility very seriously"—along with a copy of the department's antidiscrimination policy.

Methodological Appendix

1. Becker 1982.

2. Babbie 2004; Patton 2002.

3. A few artists did not nominate pseudonyms, and preferred that I use their real names. I have, unfortunately, not been able to do so, thanks to institutional review board requirements. You know who you are.

4. For example, Brooks 2002; Bureau of Labor Statistics, U.S. Department of Labor 2011; Strategic National Arts Alumni Project 2011; Throsby 2010.

5. For example, Carson 2012; Hausman 2012; de Meijer et al. 2010.

6. This should come as no surprise to ethnographers.

7. Archer 1985.

8. Wenger 1998.

9. Dewalt and Dewalt 2002; Lofland and Lofland 1995.

10. See my dissertation (Gerber 2015) for interview schedules.

11. Institutet för Konstnärer och Konstförmedlare (The Institute for Artists and Art Mediators).

12. Glaser and Strauss 1967; Strauss 1987.
13. Timmermans and Tavory 2012.
14. Becker 1976; Glaser and Strauss 1967.
15. See Gerber 2015 for codebooks and categorical codes.

Bibliography

Abbott, Andrew. 1981. "Status and Status Strain in the Professions." *American Journal of Sociology* 86(4):819–35.

Abbott, Andrew. 1983. "Professional Ethics." *American Journal of Sociology* 88(5): 855–85.

Abbott, Andrew Delano. 1988. *The System of Professions: An Essay on the Division of Expert Labor.* Chicago: University of Chicago Press.

Adams, Julia. 2005. "The Rule of the Father: Patriarchy and Patrimonialism in Early Modern Europe." Pp. 237–66 in *Max Weber's Economy and Society: A Critical Companion,* edited by C. Camic, P. S. Gorski, and D. M. Trubek. Stanford, CA: Stanford University Press.

Akerlof, George A. and Rachel E. Kranton. 2010. *Identity Economics: How Our Identities Shape Our Work, Wages, and Well-Being.* Princeton, NJ: Princeton University Press.

Almeling, Rene. 2007. "Selling Genes, Selling Gender: Egg Agencies, Sperm Banks, and the Medical Market in Genetic Material." *American Sociological Review* 72(3):319–40.

Amos, Emma. 1968. "Oral History Interview with Emma Amos, 1968 October 3." Archives of American Art, Smithsonian Institution.

Amundson, Dale. 1982. "New York New York New York . . . Copyright and More from the CIAGP Conference in New York." *CARFAC News* 7(1):10–11.

Anteby, Michel. 2010. "Markets, Morals, and Practices of Trade: Jurisdictional Disputes in the U.S. Commerce in Cadavers." *Administrative Science Quarterly* 55(4):606–38.

Archer, Margaret S. 1985. "The Myth of Cultural Integration." *British Journal of Sociology* 36(3):333–53.

"Art for Art's Sake: Its Fallacy and Viciousness." 1917. *The Art World: A Monthly for the Public Devoted to the Higher Ideals* 2(2):98–102.

Art Workers' Coalition. 1969a. *Documents 1.* New York: Art Workers' Coalition.

Art Workers' Coalition. 1969b. *Open Hearing.* New York: Art Workers' Coalition.

Aspers, Patrik. 2009. "Knowledge and Valuation in Markets." *Theory and Society* 38(2):111–31.

Babbie, Earl. 2004. *Practice of Social Research*. 10th ed. Belmont, CA: Wadsworth.

Backman, Camilla, Kajsa Dahlberg, Emma Reichert, and Isabell Dahlberg. 2006. "Ett gemensamt ansvar—ett inlägg i debatten om avtal." Retrieved May 28, 2009 (http://web.archive.org/web/20080201062028/ikk.nu/wiki/index.php/Ett_gemen samt_ansvar-_ett_inl%C3%A4gg_i_debatten_om_avtal_%282006-12-08%29).

Bain, Alison. 2005. "Constructing an Artistic Identity." *Work, Employment and Society* 19(1):25–46.

Bandelj, Nina. 2012. "Relational Work and Economic Sociology." *Politics & Society* 40(2):175–201.

Banks, Patricia Ann. 2012. "Cultural Socialization in Black Middle-Class Families." *Cultural Sociology* 6(1):61–73.

Battani, Marshall. 1999. "Organizational Fields, Cultural Fields and Art Worlds: The Early Effort to Make Photographs and Make Photographers in the 19th-Century United States of America." *Media, Culture & Society* 21(5):601–26.

Baxandall, Michael. 1972. *Painting and Experience in Fifteenth Century Italy; a Primer in the Social History of Pictorial Style*. Oxford: Clarendon Press.

Becher, Debbie. 2014. *Private Property and Public Power: Eminent Domain in Philadelphia*. Oxford: Oxford University Press.

Becker, Howard S. 1976. *Sociological Work: Method and Substance*. New Brunswick, NJ: Transaction.

Becker, Howard Saul. 1982. *Art Worlds*. Berkeley: University of California Press.

Bell-Villada, Gene H. 1986. "The Idea of Art for Art's Sake: Intellectual Origins, Social Conditions, and Poetic Doctrine." *Science & Society* 50(4):415–39.

Berman, Elizabeth Popp. 2006. "Before the Professional Project: Success and Failure at Creating an Organizational Representative for English Doctors." *Theory and Society* 35(2):157–91.

Berner, Annelie, Brian House, and Jeff Warren. 2013. "Art Degree Recipients per Year, 1987–2012." *BFAMFAPhD*. Retrieved May 26, 2016 (http://bfamfaphd.com/projects/art-degrees-per-year/).

Beveridge, Karl. 2005. "The Hidden Costs of Public Exhibitions: Artists Donate $4,000,000 a Year to the Costs of Public Exhibitions in Canada for Preparation and Installation Work." *CARFAC News* (Calendar) 8(1):4–5.

Biernacki, Richard. 1995. *The Fabrication of Labor: Germany and Britain, 1640–1914*. Berkeley: University of California Press.

Bishop, Claire. 2004. "Antagonism and Relational Aesthetics." *October* (110):51–79.

Boltanski, Luc and Laurent Thévenot. 1999. "The Sociology of Critical Capacity." *European Journal of Social Theory* 2(3):359–77.

Boltanski, Luc and Laurent Thévenot. 2006. *On Justification: Economies of Worth*. Princeton: Princeton University Press.

Bourdieu, Pierre. 1984. *Distinction: A Social Critique of the Judgement of Taste*. Cambridge, MA: Harvard University Press.

Bourdieu, Pierre. 1985. "The Market of Symbolic Goods." *Poetics* 14(1–2):13–44.

Bourdieu, Pierre. 1993. *The Field of Cultural Production: Essays on Art and Literature*. Cambridge: Polity Press.

Bourriaud, Nicolas. 2002. *Relational Aesthetics*. Paris: Les presses du réel.

Brain, David. 1991. "Practical Knowledge and Occupational Control: The Professionalization of Architecture in the United States." *Sociological Forum* 6(2):239–68.

Brante, Thomas. 2011. "Professions as Science-Based Occupations." *Professions and Professionalism* 1(1) (https://journals.hioa.no/index.php/pp/article/view/147 /143).

Brooks, Arthur C. 2002. "Artists as Amateurs and Volunteers." *Nonprofit Management & Leadership* 13(1):5.

Bryan-Wilson, Julia. 2009. *Art Workers: Radical Practice in the Vietnam War Era*. Berkeley: University of California Press.

Bunderson, J. Stuart and Jeffery A. Thompson. 2009. "The Call of the Wild: Zookeepers, Callings, and the Double-Edged Sword of Deeply Meaningful Work." *Administrative Science Quarterly* 54(1):32–57.

Bureau of Labor Statistics. 2011. *Occupational Outlook Handbook, 2010–11*. Washington, DC: U.S. Department of Labor.

Burwick, Frederick. 2001. *Mimesis and Its Romantic Reflections*. University Park: Pennsylvania State University.

Burwick, Frederick. 2014. *Romanticism: Keywords*. Hoboken: Wiley.

California College of the Arts. 2014. "Social Practice Workshop: California College of the Arts." Retrieved February 26, 2014 (https://www.cca.edu/academics/ graduate/fine-arts/socialpractices).

Carnegie Mellon University. 2014. "MFA Contextual Practice—School of Art—Carnegie Mellon University." Retrieved February 26, 2014 (http://www.cmu.edu/art/ programs/mfa/contextual-practice/).

Carson, Richard T. 2012. "Contingent Valuation: A Practical Alternative When Prices Aren't Available." *Journal of Economic Perspectives* 26(4):27–42.

Caves, Richard E. 2003. "Contracts between Art and Commerce." *Journal of Economic Perspectives* 17(2):73–84.

Chambers, Jack. 1973. "Encounters." *Canadian Artists' Representation National Newsletter*, 38–46.

Chambers, Jack, Kim Ondaatje, and Tony Urquhart. 1973. "C.A.R . . . ?" *Canadian Artists' Representation National Newsletter* 1(1):2–3.

Childress, C. Clayton. 2012. "Decision-Making, Market Logic and the Rating Mindset: Negotiating BookScan in the Field of US Trade Publishing." *European Journal of Cultural Studies* 15(5):604–20.

Childress, Clayton. 2017. *Under the Cover: The Creation, Production, and Reception of a Novel*. Princeton, NJ: Princeton University Press.

Childress, Clayton and Alison Gerber. 2015. "The MFA in Creative Writing: The Uses of a 'Useless' Credential." *Professions and Professionalism* 5(2) (https://journals.hioa.no/index.php/pp/article/view/868).

Chua, Wai-Fong and Stewart Clegg. 1990. "Professional Closure: The Case of British Nursing." *Theory and Society* 19(2):135–72.

Ciofalo, Andrew and Kim Traverso. 1994. "Does the Op-Ed Page Have a Chance to Become a Public Forum?" *Newspaper Research Journal* 15(4):51.

Cobble, Dorothy Sue. 1999. "'A Spontaneous Loss of Enthusiasm': Workplace Feminism and the Transformation of Women's Service Jobs in the 1970s." *International Labor and Working-Class History* 56(1):23–44.

Coleman, Karen. 2016. "Habermas and Art: Beyond Distinction." *American Journal of Cultural Sociology* 4(2):157–95.

Conner, Bruce. 1974. "Oral History Interview with Bruce Conner, 1974 March 29." Archives of American Art, Smithsonian Institution.

Cowen, Tyler and Alexander Tabarrok. 2000. "An Economic Theory of Avant-Garde and Popular Art, or High and Low Culture." *Southern Economic Journal* 67(2):232–53.

Crane, Diana. 1989. *The Transformation of the Avant-Garde: The New York Art World, 1940–1985.* Chicago: University of Chicago Press.

Daniels, Arlene Kaplan. 1985. "Good Times and Good Works: The Place of Sociability in the Work of Women Volunteers." *Social Problems* 32(4):363–74.

Daniels, Arlene Kaplan. 1987. "Invisible Work." *Social Problems* 34(5):403–15.

Davis, Ben. 2013. *9.5 Theses on Art and Class.* Chicago: Haymarket Books.

Day, Anita and Guy Golan. 2005. "Source and Content Diversity in Op-Ed Pages: Assessing Editorial Strategies in *The New York Times* and the *Washington Post.*" *Journalism Studies* 6(1):61–71.

de Meijer, Claudine, Werner Brouwer, Marc Koopmanschap, Bernard van den Berg, and Job van Exel. 2010. "The Value of Informal Care—a Further Investigation of the Feasibility of Contingent Valuation in Informal Caregivers." *Health Economics* 19(7):755–71.

Dewalt, Kathleen M. and Billie R. Dewalt. 2002. *Participant Observation: A Guide for Fieldworkers.* Walnut Creek, CA: AltaMira Press.

Disch, Lisa J. and Jean M. O'Brien. 2007. "Innovation Is Overtime: An Ethical Analysis of 'Politically Committed' Academic Labor." Pp. 140–67 in *Feminist Waves, Feminist Generations: Life Stories from the Academy,* edited by H. K. Aikau, K. A. Erickson, and J. L. Pierce. Minneapolis: University of Minnesota Press.

Elderfield, John, ed. 2011. *De Kooning: A Retrospective.* New York: Museum of Modern Art.

Entwistle, Joanne. 2002. "The Aesthetic Economy: The Production of Value in the Field of Fashion Modelling." *Journal of Consumer Culture* 2(3):317–39.

Espeland, Wendy Nelson and Mitchell L. Stevens. 1998. "Commensuration as a Social Process." *Annual Review of Sociology* 24:313–43.

Esping-Andersen, Gøsta. 1990. *The Three Worlds of Welfare Capitalism.* Princeton,
NJ: Princeton University Press.

Evans, James A., Gideon Kunda, and Stephen R. Barley. 2004. "Beach Time, Bridge
Time, and Billable Hours: The Temporal Structure of Technical Contracting."
Administrative Science Quarterly 49(1):1–38.

Evetts, Julia. 2003. "The Construction of Professionalism in New and Existing Occupational Contexts: Promoting and Facilitating Occupational Change." *International Journal of Sociology and Social Policy* 23(4/5):22–35.

Ewald, Johnny. 2002. "Konstnären skall ha ersättning för sitt arbete." *Konstnären*
18(2):1.

Farrell, Michael P. 2001. *Collaborative Circles: Friendship Dynamics and Creative
Work.* Chicago: University of Chicago Press.

Fine, Gary Alan. 1996. "Justifying Work: Occupational Rhetorics as Resources in
Restaurant Kitchens." *Administrative Science Quarterly* 41(1):90–115.

Fine, Gary Alan. 2003. "Crafting Authenticity: The Validation of Identity in Self-
Taught Art." *Theory and Society* 32(2):153–80.

Finkelpearl, Tom. 2000. *Dialogues in Public Art.* Cambridge, MA: MIT Press.

Fischl, Richard Michael. 2004. "A Woman's World: What If Care Work Were So-
cialized and Police & Fire Protection Left to Individual Families?" *Buffalo Law
Review* 52:659–77.

Foucault, Michel. 1972. *The Archaeology of Knowledge and the Discourse on Language.*
New York: Pantheon Books.

Fourcade, Marion. 2011. "Cents and Sensibility: Economic Valuation and the Nature
of 'Nature.'" *American Journal of Sociology* 116(6):1721–77.

Franssen, Thomas and Giselinde Kuipers. 2013. "Coping with Uncertainty, Abun-
dance and Strife: Decision-Making Processes of Dutch Acquisition Editors in the
Global Market for Translations." *Poetics* 41(1):48–74.

Fraser, Andrea. 1997. "What's Intangible, Transitory, Mediating, Participatory, and
Rendered in the Public Sphere?" *October* 80:111–16.

Freidson, Eliot. 1986. *Professional Powers: A Study of the Institutionalization of Formal Knowledge.* Chicago: University of Chicago Press.

Freidson, Eliot. 2001. *Professionalism: The Third Logic.* Chicago: University of Chicago Press.

Friedenthal, Richard. 1963. *Letters of the Great Artists.* New York: Random House.

Friedland, Roger and Robert Alford. 1991. "Bringing Society Back In: Symbols, Practices and Institutional Contradictions." Pp. 232–63 in *The New Institutionalism in
Organizational Analysis,* edited by W. Powell and P. Dimaggio. Chicago: University of Chicago Press.

Frutkin, Mark. 1987. "Copyright: From Beginning to End." *Art Action,* 2–3.

Gan, Anne Marie, Zannie Giraud Voss, Lisa Phillips, Christine Anagnos, and Alison
    D. Wade. 2014. *The Gender Gap in Art Museum Directorships*. New York: Associa-
    tion of Art Museum Directors.
Gerber, Alison. 2014a. "The Audit of Venus." *Berkeley Journal of Sociology* 58(1):6–13.
Gerber, Alison. 2014b. "Bad Art Is Good for Us All." *The Enemy* 1(3). Retrieved Sep-
    tember 24, 2014 (http://theenemyreader.org/bad-art-good-us/).
Gerber, Alison. 2014c. "The Nightmare Audit of an Indie Artist." *Narratively*. Retrieved
    March 21, 2016 (http://narrative.ly/the-nightmare-audit-of-an-indie-artist/).
Gerber, Alison. 2015. "Art Work? Tradition, Rationalization, and the Valuation of
    Contemporary Artistic Practice." Yale University (dissertation).
Gerber, Alison and Clayton Childress. 2017a. "The Economic World Obverse: Free-
    dom through Markets after Arts Education." *American Behavioral Scientist*.
Gerber, Alison and Clayton Childress. 2017b. "I Don't Make Objects, I Make Proj-
    ects: Selling Things and Selling Selves in Contemporary Artmaking." *Cultural
    Sociology*.
Glaser, Barney G. and Anselm L. Strauss. 1967. *The Discovery of Grounded Theory:
    Strategies for Qualitative Research*. Chicago: Aldine.
Golan, Guy J. 2010. "Editorials, Op-Ed Columns Frame Medical Marijuana Debate."
    Newspaper Research Journal 31(3):50–61.
Goldberg, Chad Alan. 2007. *Citizens and Paupers: Relief, Rights, and Race, from the
    Freedmen's Bureau to Workfare*. Chicago: University of Chicago Press.
Goldwater, Robert and Marc Treves, eds. 1945. *Artists on Art: From the XIV to the XX
    Century*. New York: Pantheon.
Gordon, Beverly. 2006. *The Saturated World: Aesthetic Meaning, Intimate Objects,
    Women's Lives, 1890–1940*. Knoxville: University of Tennessee Press.
Gordy, Bill. 1969. "Untitled Statement." Pp. 97–98 in *Open Hearing*. New York: Art
    Workers' Coalition.
Graw, Isabelle. 2010. *High Price: Art between the Market and Celebrity Culture*. Stern-
    berg Press.
Grusky, David B. and Kim A. Weeden. 2001. "Decomposition without Death: A Re-
    search Agenda for a New Class Analysis." *Acta Sociologica* 44(3):203–18.
Guérard, Albert. 1936. "Art for Art's Sake." *Books Abroad* 10(3):263–65.
Halperin, Julia. 2012. "Glenn Ligon and Coco Fusco among Hundreds on Petition
    Criticizing NYT Art Reviews." *Blouin Artinfo*. Retrieved May 26, 2016 (http://
    blogs.artinfo.com/artintheair/2012/11/27/glenn-ligon-and-coco-fusco-among
    -hundreds-on-petition-criticizing-nyt-art-reviews/).
Harding, David. 1997. "Public Art—Contentious Term and Contested Practice." Pp.
    9–18 in *Decadent: Public Art: Contentious Term and Contested Practice*, edited by
    D. Harding and P. Buchler. Glasgow: Foulis Press.
Hardy, K8. 2008. "Intro to W.A.G.E/Transcript of Speeches." Retrieved May 11, 2010
    (http://wageforwork.com/WAGE_RAGE_08.pdf).

Harp, Dustin, Ingrid Bachmann, and Jaime Loke. 2014. "Where Are the Women? The Presence of Female Columnists in U.S. Opinion Pages." *Journalism and Mass Communication Quarterly* 91(2):289–307.

Harrison, Charles and Paul Wood, eds. 2003. *Art in Theory 1900–2000: An Anthology of Changing Ideas*. Malden, MA: Blackwell.

Hausman, Jerry. 2012. "Contingent Valuation: From Dubious to Hopeless." *Journal of Economic Perspectives* 26(4):43–56.

Haynes, Deborah J. 1997. *The Vocation of the Artist*. Cambridge: Cambridge University Press.

Healy, Kieran. 2004. "Altruism as an Organizational Problem: The Case of Organ Procurement." *American Sociological Review* 69(3):387–404.

Healy, Kieran Joseph. 2006. *Last Best Gifts: Altruism and the Market for Human Blood and Organs*. Chicago: University of Chicago Press.

Heinich, Nathalie. 1996. *The Glory of Van Gogh: An Anthropology of Admiration*. Princeton, NJ: Princeton University Press.

Hess, Thomas B. 1962. *Recent Paintings by Willem de Kooning*. (Exhibition catalogue.) New York: Sidney Janis Gallery.

Hochschild, Arlie Russell. 1997. *The Time Bind: When Work Becomes Home and Home Becomes Work*. New York: Henry Holt.

Hochschild, Arlie Russell. 2003. *The Second Shift*. New York: Penguin.

Hyde, Lewis. 1983. *The Gift: Imagination and the Erotic Life of Property*. New York: Vintage.

Jahoda, Susan, Blair Murphy, Vicky Virgin, and Caroline Woolard. 2014. *Artists Report Back: A National Study on the Lives of Arts Graduates and Working Artists*. BFAMFAPhD.

James, Geoffrey. 1978. "Copyright & You." *CARFAC News*, 7–24.

Jenkins, Iredell. 1973. "Art for Art's Sake." Pp. 108–11 in *Dictionary of the History of Ideas: Studies of Selected Pivotal Ideas*, edited by P. P. Wiener. New York: Scribner.

Jerolmack, Colin and Shamus Khan. 2014. "Talk Is Cheap: Ethnography and the Attitudinal Fallacy." *Sociological Methods & Research* 43(2): 178–209.

Karpik, Lucien. 2010. *Valuing the Unique: The Economics of Singularities*. Princeton, NJ: Princeton University Press.

Karttunen, Sari. 1998. "How to Identify Artists? Defining the Population for 'Status-of-the-Artist' Studies." *Poetics* 26(1):1–19.

Kemp, Martin. 1997. *Behind the Picture: Art and Evidence in the Italian Renaissance*. New Haven, CT: Yale University Press.

Konstnärsnämnden. 2016a. *Årsredovisning 2015*. Stockholm: Konstnärsnämnden.

Konstnärsnämnden. 2016b. "Utdelade stipendier och bidrag 2015." Retrieved October 6, 2016 (http://www.konstnarsnamnden.se/default.aspx?id=11149).

Kopytoff, Igor. 1986. "The Cultural Biography of Things: Commoditization as Process." Pp. 64–91 in *The Social Life of Things: Commodities in Cultural Perspective*, edited by A. Appadurai. Cambridge: Cambridge University Press.

Lacy, Suzanne. 1995. *Mapping the Terrain: New Genre Public Art*. Seattle, WA: Bay Press.

Lamont, Michèle. 2012. "Toward a Comparative Sociology of Valuation and Evaluation." *Annual Review of Sociology* 38(1):201–21.

Larson, Magali Sarfatti. 1977. *The Rise of Professionalism: A Sociological Analysis*. Berkeley: University of California Press.

Leijonhielm, Maria. 1987. "'Ingen skillnad mellan rörmokare och konstnärer': Bisse Thofelt i fejd om utställningsersättningen." Pp. 4–5 in *Konstnären (1985)*, vol. 1987:3. Stockholm: Konstnärernas riksorganisation (KRO).

Lena, Jennifer C. and Danielle J. Lindemann. 2014. "Who Is an Artist? New Data for an Old Question." *Poetics* 43:70–85.

LeWitt, Sol. 1969. "Untitled Statement." Pp. 54–55 in *Open Hearing*. New York: Art Workers' Coalition.

Lofland, John and Lyn H. Lofland. 1995. *Analyzing Social Settings: A Guide to Qualitative Observation and Analysis*. 3rd ed. Belmont, CA: Wadsworth.

Lozano, Lee. 2009. *Lee Lozano: Notebooks 1967–70*. New York: Primary Information.

Luxton, Meg. 1980. *More Than a Labour of Love: Three Generations of Women's Work in the Home*. Toronto: Women's Press.

Martin, Courtney. 2011. "An Ego of One's Own." *The American Prospect*, May 13. Retrieved May 26, 2016 (http://prospect.org/article/ego-ones-own).

Mears, Ashley. 2011. *Pricing Beauty: The Making of a Fashion Model*. Berkeley: University of California Press.

Mears, Ashley. 2015. "Girls as Elite Distinction: The Appropriation of Bodily Capital." *Poetics* 53:22–37.

Menger, Pierre-Michel. 1999. "Artistic Labor Markets and Careers." *Annual Review of Sociology* 25:541–74.

Menger, Pierre-Michel. 2001. "Artists as Workers: Theoretical and Methodological Challenges." *Poetics* 28(4):241–54.

Menger, Pierre-Michel. 2014. *The Economics of Creativity: Art and Achievement under Uncertainty*. Cambridge, MA: Harvard University Press.

Messias, Deanne K. Hilfinger, Eun-Ok Im, Aroha Page, Hanna Regev, Judith Spiers, Laurie Yoder, and Afaf Ibrahim Meleis. 1997. "Defining and Redefining Work: Implications for Women's Health." *Gender and Society* 11(3):296–323.

Mondini-Ruiz, Franco. 2004. "Oral History Interview with Franco Mondini-Ruiz, 2004 July 7–8." Archives of American Art, Smithsonian Institution.

Monroe, Gerald M. 1972. "The Artists Union of New York." *Art Journal* 32(1):17–20.

Monroe, Gerald M. 1974. "Artists as Militant Trade Union Workers during the Great Depression." *Archives of American Art Journal* 14(1):7–10.

Montias, John Michael. 1989. *Vermeer and His Milieu: A Web of Social History*. Princeton, NJ: Princeton University Press.

Moorhouse, H. F. 1987. "The 'Work' Ethic and 'Leisure' Activity: The Hot Rod in Post-War America." Pp. 237–57 in *The Historical Meanings of Work*, edited by P. Joyce. Cambridge: Cambridge University Press.

National Endowment for the Arts. 2016a. *2015 Annual Report*. Washington, DC: National Endowment for the Arts.

National Endowment for the Arts. 2016b. "Grant Announcements." Retrieved October 6, 2016 (https://www.arts.gov/grants/recent-grants/grant-announcements).

National Endowment for the Arts. 2016c. "NEA Jazz Masters." Retrieved October 6, 2016 (https://www.arts.gov/honors/jazz/publications).

National Endowment for the Arts. 2016d. "NEA National Heritage Fellowships 2015." Retrieved October 6, 2016 (https://www.arts.gov/honors/heritage/year/2015).

Nelson, Jonathan K. and Richard J. Zeckhauser. 2008. *The Patron's Payoff: Conspicuous Commissions in Italian Renaissance Art*. Princeton, NJ: Princeton University Press.

Nguyen, Trong Gia. 2009. "W.A.G.E. Against the Machine." *Art21*. Retrieved May 4, 2009 (http://blog.art21.org/2009/04/27/wage-against-the-machine/#more-4846).

Nordwall, Jan. 2005. "Utställningsersättning inget arvode utan en hyra." *Konstnären* 21(1):6.

O'Connor, Francis V. 1969. "The New Deal Art Projects in New York." *American Art Journal* 1(2):58–79.

O'Malley, Michelle. 2005. *The Business of Art: Contracts and the Commissioning Process in Renaissance Italy*. New Haven, CT: Yale University Press.

The OpEd Project. 2012. *Who Narrates the World?: The OpEd Project Byline Report*. Retrieved May 26, 2016 (http://www.theopedproject.org/index.php?option=com _content&view=article&id=817&Itemid=149).

Organisation for Economic Co-operation and Development. 2005. *Growth in Services: Fostering Employment, Productivity and Innovation*. Paris: OECD.

Otterman, Sharon. 2014. "When a Loft Is Artists-Only, Deciding Who, Officially, Is an Artist." *New York Times*, January 20.

Patton, Michael Quinn. 2002. *Qualitative Research and Evaluation Methods*. Thousand Oaks, CA: Sage.

Perreault, John. 1969. "Untitled Statement." Pp. 120–21 in *Open Hearing*. New York: Art Workers' Coalition.

Perrow, Charles. 1979. *Complex Organizations: A Critical Essay*. 2nd ed. Glenview, IL: Scott, Foresman.

Petré, Margareta. 1981. "Värdera arbetet!" *KRO Konstnären* 3(6):4–5.

Plato. 1892. *Phaedrus*. In *the Internet Classics Archive*. Retrieved December 22, 2016 (http://classics.mit.edu/Plato/phaedrus.html).

Plummer, Ken. 2002. *Telling Sexual Stories: Power, Change and Social Worlds*. London: Routledge.

Polanyi, Karl. 2001. *The Great Transformation: The Political and Economic Origins of Our Time*. 2nd ed. Boston: Beacon Press.

Princenthal, Nancy. 2013. "Prolixity and Painting." *The Brooklyn Rail*. Retrieved January 4, 2017 (http://www.brooklynrail.org/2013/03/editorsmessage/prolixity-and -painting).

Pugh, Allison J. 2013. "What Good Are Interviews for Thinking about Culture? Demystifying Interpretive Analysis." *American Journal of Cultural Sociology* 1(1):42–68.

Pugh, Allison J. 2015. *The Tumbleweed Society: Working and Caring in an Age of Insecurity*. New York: Oxford University Press.

Reichert, Emma, Camilla Backman, and Camilla Palm. 2007. "IKK." Pp. 111–13 in *Taking the Matter into Common Hands: Contemporary Art and Collaborative Practices*, edited by J. Billing, M. Lind, and L. Nilsson. London: Black Dog.

Reilly, Maura. 2015. "Taking the Measure of Sexism: Facts, Figures, and Fixes." *ARTnews*. Retrieved May 26, 2016 (http://www.artnews.com/2015/05/26/taking -the-measure-of-sexism-facts-figures-and-fixes/).

Relyea, Lane. 2013. *Your Everyday Art World*. Cambridge, MA: MIT Press.

Remington, Deborah. 1973. "Oral History Interview with Deborah Remington, 1973 May 29–July 19." Archives of American Art, Smithsonian Institution.

Revers, M. 2013. "Journalistic Professionalism as Performance and Boundary Work: Source Relations at the State House." *Journalism* 15(1):37–52.

Roberts, John. 2007. *The Intangibilities of Form: Skill and Deskilling in Art after the Readymade*. London: Verso.

Rosenberg, Harold. 1972. *The De-Definition of Art*. Chicago: University of Chicago Press.

Rosso, Brent D., Kathryn H. Dekas, and Amy Wrzesniewski. 2010. "On the Meaning of Work: A Theoretical Integration and Review." *Research in Organizational Behavior* 30:91–127.

Rubinstein, Raphael, ed. 2007. "Art Schools: A Group Crit." *Art in America* 95(5):99–113.

Ruef, Martin and W. Richard Scott. 1998. "A Multidimensional Model of Organizational Legitimacy: Hospital Survival in Changing Institutional Environments." *Administrative Science Quarterly* 43(4):877–904.

Saks, Mike. 2012. "Defining a Profession: The Role of Knowledge and Expertise." *Professions and Professionalism* 2(1) (https://journals.hioa.no/index.php/pp/article/ view/151).

Saltz, Jerry. 2007. "Where Are All the Women Artists at MoMA?" *New York Magazine*, November 26. Retrieved May 26, 2016 (http://nymag.com/arts/art/ features/40979/).

Schor, Juliet B. 2010. *Plenitude: The New Economics of True Wealth*. New York: Penguin Books.

Schor, Juliet B., Connor Fitzmaurice, Lindsey B. Carfagna, and Will Attwood-Charles. 2016. "Paradoxes of Openness and Distinction in the Sharing Economy." *Poetics* 54:66–81.

Shapira, Omer. 2014. "Nobody Goes to Art School to Make Money, so Fuck Off." Retrieved June 6, 2014 (https://medium.com/@omershapira/nobody-goes-to-art-school-to-make-money-so-fuck-off-48fee12e24c2).

Sholette, Gregory. 2010. *Dark Matter: Art and Politics in the Age of Enterprise Culture.* London: Pluto Press.

Singer, Irving. 1954. "The Aesthetics of 'Art for Art's Sake.'" *Journal of Aesthetics and Art Criticism* 12(3):343–59.

Singerman, Howard. 1999. *Art Subjects: Making Artists in the American University.* Berkeley: University of California Press.

Smith, Dorothy E. 2005. *Institutional Ethnography: A Sociology for People.* Walnut Creek, CA: AltaMira Press.

Smith, Vicki. 1997. "New Forms of Work Organization." *Annual Review of Sociology* 23:315–39.

Snyder, Benjamin H. 2013. "From Vigilance to Busyness: A Neo-Weberian Approach to Clock Time." *Sociological Theory* 31(3):243–66.

Snyder, Benjamin H. 2016. *The Disrupted Workplace: Time and the Moral Order of Flexible Capitalism.* Oxford: Oxford University Press.

Solomon, Deborah. 2001. *Jackson Pollock: A Biography.* New York: Cooper Square Press.

Spillman, Lyn. 1999. "Enriching Exchange: Cultural Dimensions of Markets." *American Journal of Economics and Sociology* 58(4):1047–71.

Spillman, Lyn. 2012. *Solidarity in Strategy: Making Business Meaningful in American Trade Associations.* Chicago: University of Chicago Press.

Star, Susan Leigh and Anselm Strauss. 1999. "Layers of Silence, Arenas of Voice: The Ecology of Visible and Invisible Work." *Computer Supported Cooperative Work* 8(1–2):9–30.

Stark, David. 2009. *The Sense of Dissonance: Accounts of Worth in Economic Life.* Princeton, NJ: Princeton University Press.

Steiner, A. L. 2008. "W.A.G.E. Rage." Retrieved May 11, 2010 (http://wageforwork.com/WAGE_RAGE_08.pdf).

Strategic National Arts Alumni Project. 2011. *Forks in the Road: The Many Paths of Arts Alumni: 2010 Findings.* Bloomington: Indiana University Center for Postsecondary Research.

Strategic National Arts Alumni Project. 2013. *An Uneven Canvas: Inequalities in Artistic Training and Careers.* Bloomington: Indiana University Center for Postsecondary Research.

Strauss, Anselm L. 1987. *Qualitative Analysis for Social Scientists.* Cambridge: Cambridge University Press.

Suttner, Georg. 1971a. "Anförande vid KRO: demonstration den 16 november 1971."
  Medlemsblad (Konstnärernas Riksorganisation) 32(6–7):5–11.
Suttner, Georg. 1971b. "Ideologisk målsättning." *Medlemsblad* (Konstnärernas Riks-
  organisation) 32(2):5–6.
Swidler, Ann. 1986. "Culture in Action: Symbols and Strategies." *American Sociologi-
  cal Review* 51(2):273–86.
Tateishi, Susan Alter. 1985. "The House That Jack Built: Fifteen Years Later." *CARFAC
  News* 10:2–6.
Thompson, E. P. 1967. "Time, Work-Discipline, and Industrial Capitalism." *Past &
  Present* (38):56–97.
Thornton, Patricia H. 2001. "Personal versus Market Logics of Control: A His-
  torically Contingent Theory of the Risk of Acquisition." *Organization Science*
  12(3):294–311.
Thornton, Patricia H. and William Ocasio. 1999. "Institutional Logics and the His-
  torical Contingency of Power in Organizations: Executive Succession in the
  Higher Education Publishing Industry, 1958–1990." *American Journal of Sociol-
  ogy* 105(3):801–43.
Throsby, David. 2010. "Economic Analysis of Artists' Behaviour: Some Current Issues." *Revue d'économie politique* 120(1):47–56.
Timmermans, Stefan. 2005. "Suicide Determination and the Professional Authority
  of Medical Examiners." *American Sociological Review* 70(2):311–33.
Timmermans, Stefan and Iddo Tavory. 2012. "Theory Construction in Qualitative
  Research from Grounded Theory to Abductive Analysis." *Sociological Theory*
  30(3):167–86.
Tokumitsu, Miya. 2014. "In the Name of Love." *Jacobin*, January. Retrieved October
  22, 2014 (https://www.jacobinmag.com/2014/01/in-the-name-of-love/).
Towse, Ruth. 1996. "Economics of Training Artists." P. 381 in *Economics of the Arts:
  Selected Essays (Contributions to Economic Analysis)*, edited by V. Ginsburgh and
  P.-M. Menger. New York: Elsevier.
Tversky, Amos and Daniel Kahneman. 1974. "Judgment under Uncertainty: Heuris-
  tics and Biases." *Science* 185(4157):1124–31.
Tversky, Amos and Daniel Kahneman. 1981. "The Framing of Decisions and the Psy-
  chology of Choice." *Science* 211(4481):453–58.
Vaisey, Stephen. 2014. "Is Interviewing Compatible with the Dual-Process Model of
  Culture?" *American Journal of Cultural Sociology* 2(1):150–58.
Vasari, Giorgio. 1987. *Lives of the Artists*. New York: Viking Penguin.
Velthuis, Olav. 2003. "Symbolic Meanings of Prices: Constructing the Value of
  Contemporary Art in Amsterdam and New York Galleries." *Theory and Society*
  32(2):181–215.
Velthuis, Olav. 2005. *Talking Prices: Symbolic Meanings of Prices on the Market for
  Contemporary Art*. Princeton, NJ: Princeton University Press.

Voon, Claire. 2016. "Anish Kapoor Gets Exclusive Rights to the World's Darkest Material [Updated]." *Hyperallergic*. Retrieved July 27, 2016 (http://hyperallergic.com/279243/anish-kapoor-gets-exclusive-rights-to-the-worlds-darkest-pigment/).

Warhol, Andy. 1991. *The Andy Warhol Diaries*, edited by Pat Hackett. New York: Warner Books.

Weber, Max. 1949. *On the Methodology of the Social Sciences*. Glencoe, IL: Free Press.

Weber, Max. 1968. *From Max Weber: Essays in Sociology*. Oxford: Oxford University Press.

Weber, Max. 1978. *Economy and Society: An Outline of Interpretive Sociology*. Berkeley: University of California Press.

Weber, Max. 2001. *The Protestant Ethic and the Spirit of Capitalism*. London: Routledge.

Wenger, Etienne. 1998. *Communities of Practice: Learning, Meaning, and Identity*. Cambridge: Cambridge University Press.

Wherry, Frederick F. 2006. "The Social Sources of Authenticity in Global Handicraft Markets: Evidence from Northern Thailand." *Journal of Consumer Culture* 6(1):5–32.

Wherry, Frederick F. 2008. "The Social Characterizations of Price: The Fool, the Faithful, the Frivolous, and the Frugal." *Sociological Theory* 26(4):363–79.

White, Harrison C. and Cynthia A. White. 1965. *Canvases and Careers: Institutional Change in the French Painting World*. New York: Wiley.

Wilcox, John. 1953. "The Beginnings of l'Art pour l'Art." *Journal of Aesthetics and Art Criticism* 11(4):360–77.

Wilensky, Harold L. 1964. "The Professionalization of Everyone?" *American Journal of Sociology* 70(2):137–58.

Wilson, Carl. 2007. *Let's Talk about Love: A Journey to the End of Taste*. New York: Continuum.

Wittkower, Rudolf and Margot Wittkower. 2007. *Born under Saturn: The Character and Conduct of Artists?: A Documented History from Antiquity to the French Revolution*. New York: New York Review of Books.

Woods, Joshua. 2015. "The Op-Ed Sociologists: The Matthew Effect in Op-Ed Publication Patterns." *American Sociologist* 46(3):356–72.

Working Artists and the Greater Economy. 2016. "Mission." Retrieved April 12, 2016 (http://www.wageforwork.com/).

Wright, Mareena McKinley. 1995. "'I Never Did Any Field Work, but I Milked an Awful Lot of Cows!': Using Rural Women's Experience to Reconceptualize Models of Work." *Gender and Society* 9(2):216–35.

Wrzesniewski, Amy and Jane E. Dutton. 2001. "Crafting a Job: Revisioning Employees as Active Crafters of Their Work." *Academy of Management Review* 26(2):179–201.

Wrzesniewski, Amy, Clark McCauley, Paul Rozin, and Barry Schwartz. 1997. "Jobs,

Careers, and Callings: People's Relations to Their Work." *Journal of Research in Personality* 31(1):21–33.

Yates, Sarah. 1983. "The Applebaum-Hébert Report: An Analysis." *CARFAC News* 8(1):2–4.

Zelizer, Viviana A. 1981. "The Price and Value of Children: The Case of Children's Insurance." *American Journal of Sociology* 86(5):1036–56.

Zelizer, Viviana A. 2000. "The Purchase of Intimacy." *Law & Social Inquiry* 25(3):817–48.

Zelizer, Viviana A. 2011. *Economic Lives: How Culture Shapes the Economy*. Princeton, NJ: Princeton University Press.

Zolberg, Vera L. 1990. *Constructing a Sociology of the Arts*. Cambridge: Cambridge University Press.

Index

CULTURE
AND
ECONOMIC
LIFE

Diverse sets of actors create meaning in markets: consumers and socially engaged actors from below; producers, suppliers, and distributors from above; and the gatekeepers and intermediaries that span these levels. Scholars have studied the interactions of people, objects, and technology; charted networks of innovation and diffusion among producers and consumers; and explored the categories that constrain and enable economic action. This series captures the many angles in which these phenomena have been investigated and serves as a high-profile forum for discussing the evolution, creation, and consequences of commerce and culture.

Behind the Laughs: Community and Inequality in Comedy
Michael P. Jeffries
2017

Freedom from Work: Embracing Financial Self-Help in the United States and Argentina
Daniel Fridman
2016

The authorized representative in the EU for product safety and compliance is:
Mare Nostrum Group
B.V Doelen 72
4831 GR Breda
The Netherlands

www.ingramcontent.com/pod-product-compliance
Lightning Source LLC
Chambersburg PA
CBHW020907180526
45163CB00007B/2656